D1789254

GOD IN CONTEXT

In the 1970s theologians in Asia and Africa showed an interest in the way different cultural contexts influenced the interpretation of Christian belief. Manifestations of contextual theologies have since appeared in many parts of the world; animated international discussion about expressions, methods and theories for contextual theology have continued with the spread of contextual theology from the South to the North. The object of these theologies is to shed new light on the concept of incarnation. How does the incarnated God act in a liberating way? Contextual theology explores awareness of the interrelatedness of God and culture.

This book surveys important concepts, positions and problems of contextual theology, dealing with different criteria for the interpretation of "context" and providing explanations of different theoretical models for contextual theology. Particular topics discussed include: the importance of place for the experience of God; a dynamic, correlative and communicative view of tradition; the approach to knowledge in contextualism and the greater right of the poor to aesthetic knowledge; human ecological formation of theology; and the contributions of pictorial art and architecture to contextual theology. Clearly explaining the importance of contextual theology for all theology, this book offers an invaluable text for students and others exploring theology in context.

God in Context
A Survey of Contextual Theology

SIGURD BERGMANN

ASHGATE

Published by
Ashgate Publishing Limited
Gower House
Croft Road
Aldershot
Hants GU11 3HR
England

Ashgate Publishing Company
Suite 420
101 Cherry Street
Burlington, VT 05401-4405
USA

Ashgate website: http://www.ashgate.com

British Library Cataloguing in Publication Data
Bergmann, Sigurd
    God in context : a survey of contextual theology. -
    1. Christianity and culture
    I. Title
    230'.046

Library of Congress Cataloging-in-Publication Data
Bergmann, Sigurd, 1956-
    God in context : a survey of contextual theology / Sigurd Bergmann.
        p. cm.
    Includes bibliographical references and index.
    ISBN 0-7546-0615-5 (alk. paper)
        1. Christianity and culture. 2. Theology–Methodology. I. Title.

    BR115.C8 B42 2003
    230–dc21

2002190896

ISBN 0 7546 0615 5

Printed and bound in Great Britain by MPG Books Ltd, Bodmin, Cornwal

Contents

List of Illustrations

Foreword

It is a privilege to be asked to write an Introduction to Sigurd Bergmann's new book on contextual theology, "God in Context". I am
always struck in my communication with the author of the significance
of context and in particular by the significance of light in his work. At
times when I have been writing in brilliant sunshine, Sigurd Bergmann
has been struggling with very few hours of daylight. The diverse ways
by which this affects mood, vision, outlook and spirituality in a real
way form the background to this book. The second strand of background is the way the spirit of the late Per Frostin is an inspirational
presence in the book. I first went to the University of Lund in Sweden in 1992, shortly after his death, and was immediately aware of the
sense of bereavement among his friends, colleagues and students of the
University. The importance of his work was explained to me by my
friend and colleague, feminist theologian Anna Karin Hammar. The
trail blazed by Per Frostin's commitment to Liberation Theology and
to the significance of context, together with the author' s conviction
that the aesthetic dimension has been lost from appreciation of this,
form a dynamic frame to "God in Context".

But, the reader may ask, how does this title operate in bringing together commitment to liberation, awareness of context, and aesthetics?
Does not "in Context" suggest merely an "attribute" of God, a method
of working, and give a much too instrumental flavour to the argument?
My own brief experience of working with Sigurd Bergmann at the International Colloquium of "Kairos Europa" (Germany 2000) made me
aware of the depth and promise of his way of working. It may be a
truism to say "all theology is contextual" – but this has not been recog-
nised until recently by the Academy. Even when taken into account, far
too little attention has been paid to the fact that the dominant context
for theology has been Eurocentric, male and rational, according to the
Enlightenment paradigm. Even when the voices of "the marginalised"
are occasionally admitted to the discussion, seldom are they given full

status; on the contrary, they are frequently relegated – yes, to the margins – on the grounds that "praxis" somehow does not merit recognition as "real theology".

"God in Context" pays full attention to the revelatory situation and to revelation in action. "In Context" captures the dynamic, communicating aspect of revelation as appealing in an integrated way to persons-in-community, to heart, mind and body. The author rightly recovers the power of symbol and image often overlooked by "tradition". Symbol, he writes, both refers and manifests. It is both metaphor of the incarnation and itself incarnates. But the argument only works because Bergmann offers an interpretation of tradition that is no mere handing on of knowledge, but is respectful of local traditions, encourages the integration of suppressed and invisible groups, gives priority to this underside and encourages ecological expressions.

In our contemporary situation – where many writers are discovering "context" – there are two unique factors to be stressed. Setting himself against the modern myth of "progress" Bergmann offers us an insightful "ecological" model of contextual theology - building on other models, yet helping the reader to understand the significance of place, nature and landscape as locus of revelation. The human being does not stand alone before God but in a complex net or web of social, ecological and culturally-defined relations. The sacredness of place is becoming popular as theme for spirituality. But "God in Context" takes us further, into the role of the senses in the revelatory experience.

Simply reading the final chapter was itself a profound experience. Bergmann brings to us in a sensitive manner four pictures from diverse contexts: N. German, N. Australia from an aboriginal perspective, Norway (a Sami perspective), and a Japanese Cross from the Hokkaido Mountains. All four are depictions of the Cross/Crucifixion. All four involve the sensuous appreciation and perception of landscape. They are a living, functional, drawing – out of the integrated understanding of knowledge that Bergmann offers us. Appealing to the experiences of poor people – often conflictual and overwhelmed by the "dark side of life" – artistic expressions, themselves selecting elements of profound significance for the community, can help us find in the landscape answers to the cry of anguish of our hearts. As Bergmann writes: "In Ando's spiritual landscape of the cross, we meet a God in function".

This book appears as the world has entered into a stage of violence that Per Frostin had neither experienced nor dreamed of. My hope is that this sensitive study can offer greater depth into the way that the Divine is experienced in the complex web of our interconnected lives.

Mary Grey, University of Wales, Lampeter

Contextual models all seek to bring something different to the other — in that endeavor the succeed — ~~but~~ each adds to the greater puzzle. But none 'solve' the puzzle.

(2) Content of Models

(1) 'Context of 'Contextual Theology' — see preface.

(3) The models
— Bevan
— Bergman

Preface

'Spaces & places'

In the beginning of the 1970s theologians in Asia and Africa took an interest in how different cultural contexts affected the interpretation of Christianity.

There were many reasons for this: growing pluralism, discontent with conventional generalizing ways of approaching theology, the need for new theological expressions in changeable cultural situations.

Expressions of contextual theologies since then emanate in many places from believers, who in fellowship reflect upon their experiences with the interaction between the God of the Gospels and traditions and the context. Strong approaches exist, among others: Latin-American liberation theology, feminist theology, African and North American black theology, Ecotheology, Minjung-, and Palestinian theology, native spirituality and in the regional "kairos processes".

At the centre of the debate about what contextual theology is and how we can shape it, stands the intention to attach greater importance to the sociocultural and sometimes also the ecological "situation" for the interpretation of the ongoing revelation of God. This intention leads contextual theology to shed a new light upon the thought of incarnation. How does God become flesh in concrete situations? How does the embodied God act in a liberating way? In accordance with the tradition of trinitarian theology the incarnation of the Son is followed by the inhabitation of the Holy Spirit, as I have learnt from Gregory of Nazianz. For contextual theology, the challenge, therefore, is to move into the spaces and places where God's Holy Spirit redeems the creatures and creation. Where do we find the habitats of the lifegiving Spirit? How do we meet "the life of the coming world"?

During the 1980s local theologies and the contextual approach as well spread from South to North. Since then there has been an intensive international discussion about expressions, methods and theories for contextual theology. In the Nordic countries, for example, the academic network "Nordic forum for contextual theology" since 1991 has renewed and transformed the agenda of systematic theology. In Germany the excellent coordination of reflections in many regions of the world should be especially mentioned which the "Theologie Interkulturell" foundation at the Catholic Faculty of Frankfurt University has developed since 1990.

In this book I give an overview of important conceptions, positions and problems in the international discussion. I treat different criteria for the interpretation of the "context" and I examine various models of contextual theology. The subtitle "a survey of" aims at the intention of offering the reader a large-scale map. With the help of this it will be possible to separate contextual theology from other theology and grasp more clearly the nuances and problems in the current state of theology. The book not only constitutes an investigative, descriptive statement, but it also offers constructive and creative proposals.

Nonetheless, the reader who expects an outworked theology in the dogmatic sense of a collection of main doctrines of "the" Christian faith will be disappointed. The content of my theological approach in this book should rather to be sought in its methodology than in a postulated dogmatic content. The way of approaching theology should in itself be regarded as a genuine theological expression and argument. Because of God's ongoing liberating revelation for others and us, and because the God of the believers is a God of their Here and Now, the method of theology carries its message. The book wants to encourage the contextualization of theology from below as a manifold, polycentric and transcultural reflection on and expression of the acting God in both well-known and still unknown places.

The first chapter gives a preliminary definition of the notion "contextual theology" and discusses why theology today ought to be contextual.

A person who wants to attach greater importance to the context for the reflection on God should define what is meant by "context". In the second chapter, I therefore treat ten dimensions in the context and describe different ways of approaching theology.

In a third step, special attention is given the importance of tradition of contextual theology, as this is mainly oriented towards contemporary problems. In that connection I proceed from the conviction that an interpretation of the past deepens the possibility to solve current problems. I shape a dynamic and communicative view of tradition for the correlation between tradition and context to be successful.

The fourth chapter discusses if contextual theology really offers a new view of theological reflection. In connection with the demands of the theology of liberation that the poor have precedence at the interpretation of the experience of God, and in connection with contextualism's theory of knowledge, I plead for a theological shift of paradigm, i.e. for a changeover to another way of approaching theology. The title of the book summarizes this demand. God scarcely will be found beyond but in the context. Theology's task is not the interpretation of "God in general" but the interpretation of "God in function" and "God here and today for us".

This chapter also highlights the significance that Per Frostin had for Nordic contextual history. In the tradition of the "Lund-theology" after Gustav Aulén, from which both Frostin and the author have their roots, the theology of the Church is no more or less than a human tool of God's liberation of the Creation. Academic and pastoral theology never exist for their own sake but as part of a salvation drama of the others and the whole in God's struggle against evil and for life.

Frostin became a pioneer in the field through his pastoral engagement and through his open-mindedness in his research on European political and African interpretations of Christianity. He researched critically the so-called two-regiment "doctrine" of Martin Luther and its abuse and theology's dialogue with the sociology of knowledge. This book also aims at cultivating the same field. The premature death of Per Frostin in 1992 did not, after all, result in any setback for the development of contextual theology in the Nordic countries. His death signified an irreplaceable loss of unique competence, but it also became a catalyst for others to intensify the project.

In spite of the young age of contextual theology its theoretical formation is abundant. The fifth chapter discusses the grouping of contextual theology in five different models by the American missionary scientist, Stephan B. Bevans. It also extends his diagram with a sixth, human ecological model.

In the sixth chapter we will look at pictorial art. Three paintings originating in northern German, Australian-aboriginal and Sami contexts together with a Japanese church space, are carefully interpreted as an expression of contextually image and space creating theology. In this way, theology's method of expression is widened from no longer thinking exclusively in words. The artists show in their configurations how we can experience, express and think the ongoing revelation in image and space.

The texts originated partly as lectures at a course on Contextual Theology that was arranged by the Department of Theology and Religious Studies in Lund during the autumn of 1995 and partly as contributions to scientific conferences. The third chapter is a rewritten version of a lecture delivered at the Nordic research course on the relationship between the theory and practice of contextual theology. It was arranged in June 1995 at Baroniet Rosendal at the Norwegian Hardanger fjord. The fourth chapter builds in part upon a contribution to the Nordic conference of systematic theologians in Aarhus in January 1995, and in part on a lecture delivered at the seminar "Blessed are the poor" that was arranged in the autumn of 1992 in memory of Per Frostin. The present English edition of the text has slightly been revised after its original Swedish version ("Gud i funktion") published 1997 by Verbum in Stockholm.

I wish to acknowledge above all the valuable comments of my students in Lund, Göteborg and Trondheim, as well as of Agneta Bengtsson, Lund, Ingela Bergmann, Trondheim, Ulrich Duchrow, Heidelberg, Cristina Grenholm, Karlstad, Mary Grey, Lampeter, Kjetil Hafstad, Oslo, Anna Karin Hammar, Lund, Manfred Hofmann, Lund, Werner G. Jeanrond, Lund, Tage Kurtén, Åbo, Aasulv Lande, Lund, Per Erik Persson, Lund, Lissi Rasmussen, Copenhagen, and last but not least Robert J. Schreiter, Chicago/Nijmegen. The dialogue with Per Frostin (†1992) and with the colleagues at the symposia of our Nordic Forum on Contextual Theology and at the symposia of the Foundation "Theologie Interkulturell" in Frankfurt am Main were particularly significant in the development of the lines of thought that lead to this book. An acknowledgment of a kind where words no longer do is given to my sensitive translator Anna Bielke Komorowska, Trondheim, as well as to Stewart Clark for his editing and Jan Komorowski who assisted her. The translation of the book was made possible through a contribution from the Research Council of Norway in Oslo and its final editing was professionally and smoothly accomplished by the publisher Sarah Lloyd.

Trondheim

Sigurd Bergmann

Chapter 1

The Challenge to Theology

Theology today ought to be contextual theology.

This thesis moves us immediately into the centre of the ongoing debate about whether theology is necessary in the so-called postmodern society? If the answer is yes, is there only one correct way or several different equally correct ways of approaching theology? How is it possible to model theology with universal claims of validity? How do different conditions of social, cultural, historical, and ecological nature influence meditation over the meeting with God?

These questions keep returning if one looks at the list of publications in academic and theological debate. Several possible answers may be discerned. The same questions occur in the pastoral sphere as well. Here we have discussions about issues like, the process of self-examination in the Swedish Lutheran church, the Roman Catholic world catechism, theology of liberation and the validity of feminist theology, all of which show a fragmentary, changeable, and conflict-filled picture of standpoints.

In Sweden, one question has been posed for a long time: is it at all possible to draw any relevant conclusions about the belief in God as a shaper of society? The question is whether the claims of theology convince others than those who have already found salvation? The result is that many members of the clergy and theologians either retire to exclusively confessional language or prefer arguments, supposedly shared by all mankind, about theology. A simple solution is to switch between the two languages: to talk religiously about and to God with confessors and to talk generally about God with others. Whether a naturalistic or an economic outlook on the world is considered, the humanist's perspective on life will be as problematic as the perspective of the Christian faith when related to the development of the postmodern image of the world.

This means, is it possible to meditate on God in the middle of different events in life or should this only be reserved for confessions behind closed doors? Where and how will a theological text become meaningful? Should one promote a non-confessional language for the Christian faith?

This first chapter summarizes the reasons which support the argument that theology ought to be contextual in today's post-modern society. First, I will outline the meaning of the notion and its history and define the difference between "contextual" and "non-contextual" theology. Then I will give six reasons for contextualization of the Christian interpretation of life. "To contextualize" means to heighten the consciousness of the significance of the context of thinking and acting.

What is "Contextual Theology"?

"Context" is an immigrant from philology. It refers to that which surrounds (Latin con-) a text. Context means the parts of a text that precede and follow the text in question and which are of importance for its understanding.

The words "time (Greek kairos) is now" are preceded, for instance, in the Gospel of St Mark by the information about the arrest of John the Baptist and Jesus' voyage to Galilee. The narrative follows the text where the disciples are called to be fishers of men and women. The text about kairos has a context. It denotes a particular political situation where the prophet finds himself in conflict with the governing powers. The text is also inserted in a context of action from which arises the first fellowship around Christ. This is the foundation of the later church. The further context of this text is decided by the classical collection of texts "The Bible" which the young church's canonical decision granted a normative function for the fellowship of faith.

The linguistic meaning of context can be transferred to other fields. Today the word also denotes the particular social, cultural and ecological situation within which a course of events takes place. A theological text, for instance, comes into being within a wider context, that is, it is determined by the traditions and circumstances that have an effect on the complex situation of the author and the reader.[1] The text is also dependent on a connection with other texts. The meaning of the text originates in what can be termed "intertextuality".

The text and the context interact in two directions. This can be modelled as the circle of function. The interpretation of Christianity's shape and content interacts with a large number of factors in the context within which they are created.

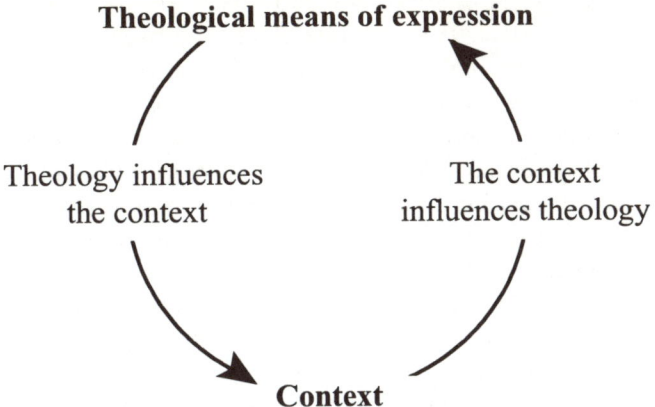

Theological means of expression

Theology influences
the context

The context
influences theology

Context

Figure 1.1: The "circle of function" between theological expression and
contex

The history of the notion of context is short. Two Asiatic theologians, Shoki Coe and Aharon Sapsezian, pleaded in 1973 for a contextualization of theology.[2] They then demanded that the educational
programme of the ecumenical movement should take place in context,
that is, theological education should be brought into "the field" to a
larger degree. Theology should be a living meeting between a universal
Gospel and the specific reality where people are.

During the 1970s and 1980s a large number of programmed attempts
were made where human experiences in particular situations were given
a central function in theology. This was done without employing the
designation "contextual theology". Special attention was given to experiences of suffering and structurally conditioned repression.

The theology of liberation arose in Latin America as a people's
evangelization among primary groups. It was a reflection of the significance of faith in God for a people's fight for freedom from an unjust
dependence upon colonial powers.[3] In black theology, theologians in
Africa and the USA focused upon the experience of being black and
marginalized.[4] The Minjung theology in Korea brought the suffering
people's pain into theological focus.

Since then, feminist theology has treated the issue of how women
and men will understand God's historical and present revelation in a
multi-faceted manner. This is in relation to biologically and socially
constructed conceptions of gender. The latest addition is ecological
theology, which since 1972 has grown as a theological reflection on ex-

perience by nature conservationist and urban green movements based on modern society's destructive relations to nature.

In spite of contextual theology coming into being already in 1973, it was not until the 1990s that it was applied in relation to all these approaches. The notion of contextual theology today also functions as a means of gathering the theological approaches that emanate from a similar understanding of theology's task and method. Contextual theologians are also noted for striving to interpret what I will call "the ongoing incarnation". They have a unifying trait in that they depart from people's specific experiences in their meetings with God in unique situations. The conditions that are clear beforehand, such as conditions of support, the physical space, the language, ways of thinking, form of culture, traditions, are given a leading and fundamental significance by contextual theologians in the interpretation of the acts of God.

We can therefore distinguish between two characteristics in the notion of contextual theology. First, it aims at a theological method. Contextual theology is an interpretation of Christian faith, which arises in the consciousness of its context. The interpretation of "God today"[5] occurs in connection and in dialogue with people, phenomena and traditions in our age and the surrounding world. Contextual theology not only gathers the experiences that arise in specific situations. It also strives to actively change the context. In this way, theology becomes part of the process of cultural renewal. Text and context, theological and cultural contents and shapes of expression, all interact in two directions in a common circle of function.

Second, the notion indicates a group of attempts, which in different circumstances use and develop this method.[6] The common traits in these attempts can be listed as follows:

- the significance of the subject's specific experiences, in particular experiences of suffering and deliverance,

- the criticism of the theology of eternity and the confusion between local and universal claims to validity,

- the striving for social and emancipating relevance,

- the renewal of theological ways of expression in close collaboration with local forms of culture,

- the assumption of the unity of the world and history caused by belief in the Creation and a positive estimation of cultural and biological multitude in the wholeness of Creation.

True universality can only be achieved when all collectively learn from each other & assimilate other's lessons, treasures as our own.

The Challenge to Theol/

"Contextual theology" also encompasses two different though related areas of action in the pastoral and academic spheres. The main figures in the church shape the rendering of the Christian faith in accordance with its context for pastoral theology. In academic theology, the main figures of science reflect upon connections between the rendering of the Christian faith and the context.

Apart from contextual theology, there are also discussions about contextualization, meaning a conscious process in which theology focuses on the importance of context.

Contextual and Non-Contextual Theology

Contextual theology is therefore understood as the interpretation of Christian faith which is conscious of the importance of the situation and connection for shaping the theology.

It is, of course, possible to opt for another definition and assert, for example, that contextual theology is different from universal theology. This would then make contextual theology into the kind of interpretation of the Christian faith that arises in a special context, for example, the poor in the Dalit caste in India or the Christian minority in China. Such a theology is considered to be completely determined by its context, which brings it into opposition with a universal theology, meaning an interpretation of the Christian faith, which is valid for all Christians in the world. Contextual would then mean being "determined by context" and its opposite would be "theology that is independent of context".

The representatives of contextual theology claim, however, that every theology is determined by its context. This means that there are no universal theologies, which work independently of their context. Per Frostin claims that one should distinguish between interpretations of the Christian faith that are conscious of context and those that are not, rather than differentiating between context-dependent and context-independent.[7]

Robert J. Schreiter suggests that we should also distinguish between "local theologies" and "contextual theologies". According to him, local theology indicates those interpretations of the Christian faith that arise among believers in a certain place. On the contrary, by using the notion contextual theology we focus upon a sensitivity for and consciousness of the importance of the social and cultural connections.[8] In this way, different local theologies can be more or less sensitive to and conscious of the importance of context.

Perhaps in trying to define contextual theology has a tendency to see the specifics of an individual context as mutually exclusive to an overarching theology, and therefore also mutually exclusive as universal theology.

But he fails to recognize the possibility that individual theologies are part of a universal collective. & "our thinking of God & Christ are incomplete while pieces of the puzzle are missing.

If by this we mean that every theology today must be contextual, it then signifies an inevitable demand upon the consciousness of the respective interpretations of the Christian faiths and their contexts. Whoever expresses a selection of statements of faith and asserts their normative value for others must be able to account for a number of questions. When, where and how have these dogma arisen? Which person or which persons have formulated them? For whom are they valid? Under which circumstances are they valid?

If we say that every theology today ought to be conscious of its context this does not mean that this is something completely new exactly in our time. We could rather assert that many interpretations of the faith in the long history of theology have been contextual. This is precisely because they are consciously attached to the prerequisites of the surrounding world and the actual period.

In the Christian tradition contextual theology already exists so it does not need to be invented. Albert Nolan has consequently formulated the thesis: "All theology is contextual".[9] The innovative aspect in this is that for him theology is no longer a study of God but a study of what God says and does in a context. According to Nolan, theology is rather a study of the context per se.[10]

Naturally, one could now argue that if theology always has been contextual there is nothing new in this. Is this simply just another and awfully complicated word denoting an old truth? If the purpose is known, why cannot we just let the matter rest?

This is certainly a matter of insight that our predecessors in the history of theology also must have experienced. There is no obstacle, though, to the need of being interpreted again. As we shall see, contextual theology to a very high degree lays claim to being in harmony with the Christian tradition.

Yet, there is often another string to this objection. The critic thinks that if it really does not contain anything new, there is no reason to change known methods of shaping the interpretation of the Christian faith. The thesis, which states that modern theology must be contextual, aims at this misunderstanding.

There are several factors here which necessitate a change in thought and perspective. Methods are used that are devoid of context and are full of generalizations. In modern society, we like to perceive these as being traditional instead of asking whether in fact they are in contrast to Christian traditions rather than in harmony with them.

The question could simply be whether modern theologians have worked as if there were no contexts with women, the poor, nature, clouds, streets and children. Perhaps conventional theology has totally disregarded the fact that people have independently had religious experiences and theology in its reflection needs to take care of them. Who constructs theology? Who has credibility in a conviction of faith?

The critic, who states that contextual theology could hardly be new and therefore everything ought to stay as it is, could be answered by referring to the constant demands of revelation to interpret old knowledge once again. We can also point to several issues that reflect the state of postmodern society.

What makes it essential that theology today should necessarily be contextual? Why should the Christian interpretation of life be more aware of the context?[11]

Why Should We Contextualize the Christian Interpretation of Life?

It is possible to distinguish between several factors which make it necessary for theology to be aware of its context. There are historical, political and cultural reasons as well as factors that are fundamental to Christianity.

Criticizing the Theology of Eternity and the Demand for Relevance

The first factor is found in the common dissatisfaction with conventional ways of approaching theology. Radical criticism has been aimed at perceiving theology as an invariable, exclusive and eternal activity, a so-called "theologia perennis" or the theology of eternity. The relevance of theological practice is the central issue in this criticism.

The German theologian, Jürgen Moltmann, delivers this criticism and meets it by consequently structuring all of his books according to a pattern of "identity and relevance".[12] He is of the opinion that the interpretation of the Christian faith needs to be partly authentic, that is identical with the specific traits of Christian tradition, and partly relevant, meaning that it would be applicable in a liberating way to different situations in society. According to a term used by the North American theologian David Tracy, the theologian's task is to bring about a "correlation" between tradition and situation.[13]

At the general assembly of the World Council of Churches in 1968, the ecumenical movement expressed a relevant demand through the formula: the agenda of the world is also that of the church.

There are two important historical reasons for the criticism of the theology of the eternity and for the demand for increased theological relevance. One reason lies in the development of sociology and its signification during this century. The other reason is that the number of Christians in the South during the 1980s has exceeded the number of Christians in the North while at the same time Christian faith in the North has increasingly embroiled itself in a crisis of credibility and legitimacy.

The Sociocultural Construction of Reality

Insights from sociology show the increasing awareness of the importance of the societal context. The so-called sociology of knowledge reveals, above all, that the perception of the reality of individuals and groups always is socially determined. We talk of the social construction of reality.[14] However, there are considerable differences between various social groups and at the same time there are resemblances too. People from various social circumstances understand, think, talk and act in different ways.

Modern society's acute differentiation into compartments for work, education, generation and sex reinforces these differences even more and leads to an increased fragmentation of the understanding of realities. The conditions for meeting and speaking the same language are considerably diminished, while the media and markets of consumption with their extreme geographical outreach create new homogeneous elements in the culture of the world.

Depending on the times and the social and cultural conditions, that which seems reasonable or unreasonable is no longer a foregone conclusion. History loses its normative value. The speed of these changes is accelerating. In a small socio-geographic area there might be a varied patchwork with different patterns of rationality. That which appears to be reasonable to an owner of a business in Stockholm might be seen as completely unreasonable to a street seller in Lima, Peru.

Sociologists are of the opinion that modern society is characterized by "goal rationality" (Max Weber), in other words, that which seems reasonable and leads to reaching predestined goals. Goal rationality instrumentalizes our fellow creatures and nature to reach aims. The result dispels and eventually destroys a large number of non-instrumental values in life. In the economic interpretation of reality, it seems neither reasonable nor useful to fall in love, protect a blue-winged butterfly, or to read a novel. One could possibly justify these acts, as bringing about experiences which might in themselves be tools to achieve a happier life. In the post-modern society experiences are also rationally subordinated and instrumentalized in goal rationality, such as through tourism and the creation of haut culture.

The social sciences changed during the 20th century. Previously there was a link in the modern project, which sought to liberate the human being through the enlightenment of reason. Now social sciences are more about exploring the social and cultural conditions, which make people act as they do. It did not turn out to be quite that simple that if only man was capable of thinking reasonably, devoid of superstition and ignorance, then he would be able to solve social problems rationally and technically. The modern project failed and in Sweden criticism about the so-called art of social engineering has summed up this failure rather well. People and society turned out to be considerably more complicated than what was presumed by the worker's movement at the turn of the 20th century.

The cultural sciences attract growing interest today. Ethnology is no longer a study of antiquated folklore traditions but is a study of current forms of life. Human ecology studies the interaction between human beings and the environment. Social anthropology is no longer exclusively dedicated to peoples outside the western hemisphere in the aftermath of colonialism but studies cultural encounters and patterns of behaviour as well. Research into modernity tries to determine what distinguishes the state of modernity and how this is being transformed at present.

Production of knowledge in the social and cultural sciences is an important challenge to theology that it should no longer avoid. Sociology makes it almost impossible to disregard the fact that each human means of expression and behaviour arises in a social and cultural context. This also applies to the philosophy of life, religious notions and behaviour and forms of organization.

Given our insight into the social prerequisites of religion, the theology of eternity seems to be an illusion. The reflection over God as an expression of the experience of meeting this God is and will remain bound to the sociocultural context in which these experiences occur. The interpretation of the experience is not of course bound to the particular individual, place or point in time since we command language, memory and the ability to code and exchange patterns of thought over long periods of time. It is evident, though, that even the time-constant ways of thinking remain tied to the cultural soil in which they once could grow and thrive. From the perspective of the science of culture,

[handwritten margin note:] It is not the theology that is eternal but the 'theos' God that is eternal

we can partly differentiate between concrete prerequisites for the deter-
mination of place in context and the prerequisites of persistency and
over-dimensionality. The factors that are defined in time and place
could be called "culture" and the coded time-constant factors "tradition". A vital social cultural context always consists of these two elements functioning in the inter-subjective process of communication and
action.

This insight is very important for contextual theology if one wants
to meet the critical objection that this effort reduces Christian faith to
a faith, which can only make small, relative claims in very limited local
circumstances. Could female theology for example really say something
important to men? Does this give up the universal claims of Christianity by affirming the particular, in other words, the perspective of the
other sex? Is the idea of creation threatened if at the beginning one
perspective is given priority?

One may assert, with the help of cultural science, that there is no
opposition between the particular and the universal. The global entirety
always remains composed of many small local contexts. The problems
that exist are between different specific contexts. How should women
talk for men so as to understand and vice versa? How is it possible to
interpret the Charter of the United Nations in a similar way in Somalia
and Iraq?

The challenge to intercontextual dialogue is not a construction of
one all-extensive language but the development of rules for languages
for communication between different particular contexts. The universal
is not available for individuals or groups to claim complete knowledge.
What exists, are particular conditions for gaining knowledge of one's
own life and the life of others, as well as the general adhesion to laws
like that in the evolution process.

As humanity has the ability of transculturation, there is no opposition between tradition and local culture either. From time to time,
we are able to code and hand over insights and ways of thinking in the
medium of language and pictures. It is within our .means to convey
and share ways of thinking and information between several different
geographical cultures, all in very large spaces of time. Our new communication systems offer opportunities that were unheard of earlier. The
large amount of information, however, hampers rather than benefits the
exchange of information.

Even in relation to these systems, being deeply rooted locally is an
essential tool for being able to communicate across cultural borders.
Someone who settles in a computer network will quickly lose his ele-

mentary ability of interpreting. The indigenous populations developed a world dialogue during the 1990s which they quickly and successfully developed. With this in mind, perhaps one could try the formula: the stronger the local roots, the greater the potential for communication in translocal meetings of culture.

At the moment, the whole area of research within intercultural communication is in a very dynamic phase of development. For those who want to apply a scientific perspective to ways of expression in religion, I would like to emphasize, that insight into the nature of social and cultural contexts today is an indispensable prerequisite. To investigate content and ways of expression in the Christian faith, one can no longer bypass the context within which these means of expression obtain their purpose. Academic contextual theology strives to fulfil this demand.

The thesis that theology today ought to be contextual, therefore, aims not only at pastoral but also academic theology and, in reality, everything in Religious Studies. We might formulate its demand as a rational criterion of theology. Therefore, each scientific reflection on the worldview must comprise an investigation of its connection with the social and cultural contexts within which this worldview becomes meaningful.

Apart from sociology and cultural science, it is naturally also possible to bring forward the philosophical criticism of the idea of the modern subject, which is usually called "postmodernism". There are numerous advocates of this criticism, and therefore, I will treat it only sporadically.[15]

Hermeneutics is the science of interpreting, which takes into consideration the subject of interpretation and the specific qualifications of the reader. The above-mentioned criticism has led to academic theology today being developed as hermeneutics. In short, the postmodern criticism signifies a "deconstruction" of what Descartes meant when he wrote that man alone is a sensible thinking creature.

The postmodern criticism of the subject as being reason fixated claims to the contrary that the ego of humankind arises in a complex web of relations that are psychological, social and biological. This criticism further asserts that the modern objectivistic view of knowledge is totally invalid. Nobody can claim universal knowledge as each such construction in a discourse constitutes an aspiration for power over fellow men and objects.[16]

Are there possibilities of considering history and the planet as being homogeneous without disregarding the knowledge of the subjective and social construction of reality? The unsolved question in this philosophical discussion is if we ought to view reality as something fragmented, relativistic and atomic.

We can summarize the first reason. Because of the sociology of knowledge, cultural science and the postmodern deconstruction of power concentrated, universalistic discourses, it is necessary in pastoral and academic theology to reflect upon the importance of context for the interpretation of the Christian faith. Faith in God ought to be interpreted as a sociocultural construction in which individuals and groups put unique experiences of their encounters with a living God into words. Pastoral theology constitutes a formation of signification in this encounter. In this sense, contextual theology does not constitute any narrowing to restricted circumstances of claims to the truth of the Christian faith. On the contrary, contextual theology creates new conditions for transcultural interpretation of the Christian faith, which could win extensive validity in a global society of many cultures. Only that which appears to be credible in a local context could be the foundation of claims of universal validity.

The Faces of Christianity in the South

The second reason lies in the geographic and cultural dispersion of Christians. Christianity has its historic origins in the Third World in the African and eastern part of the Mediterranean and the faith was shaped in medieval Europe.[17] The theology that has been fundamental to Christianity's history of mission during the Colonial period has been a local European theology which the church managed to shape as an all encompassing interpretation of reality.

This Eurocentric interpretation of Christianity has also become problematic in connection with the attainment of the political freedom of the people of the South who increasingly have devoted themselves to a historic and political scrutiny of their dependence on Western Europe. The question becomes inflamed especially as the number of Christians in the South exceeds the number living in North America and Europe.

Can the Eurocentric interpretation of Christianity, which so far has successfully defended its universal validity, remain normative for Christians outside Europe? How far can the inculturation of Christianity proceed in other cultures? Which are the criteria for a Christian reading of the Bible outside of the West? Where is the border between a syncretical mixture of religions and a culturally new interpretation of the faith? Is there something which remains unchanged through all places and times, or does perhaps the Christian belief in God distinguish itself through the belief in the variability of God?

A person, who wants to keep these questions at arm's length, could beneficially push the whole problem of contextual theology over to the missionary field. This seems to be a trifle too easy, though. Criticism against Eurocentric theology's claim to universality is far too accurate for it to be dismissed as other people's problem. The discussion about the problems of inculturation poses several difficult questions also for the theology of the West.

Are not the interpretations of Christianity by Thomas, Luther and Barth as intertwined with their culture as Minjung theology, the theology of liberation and Black theology today? What triggers the discovery that western theology has absorbed the patriarchal view of the human person and the instrumental view of nature?

There are three reasons for not referring contextual theology to the missionary field:

– The criticism against western theology's claim to universality is devastating. On the other hand, if one receives this criticism it leads to a new humbleness towards one's own local history.

– Western theology has in an unreflecting way embedded itself in the Eurocentric, patriarchal, colonistic and anthropocentric ideology. Therefore a radical examination of the results of this embedding is needed.

– The cultural identity of the West during this century is no longer constructed using the Christian belief in God. The Christians find themselves, therefore, in a missionary situation.

This is why there is a need for a new, different Christian interpretation of a way of life which is better integrated in changed social circumstances.

The Ongoing Modernization of the State of Society

The third reason lies in the sweeping changes in the social and cultural reality of modern society.

These changes can be summarized as modernization. Through urbanization, technology, internationalization and industrialization modern society has created new patterns of production and reproduction, which is an ecological revolution.[18] Modern industrial society creates cultural life forms, manners and lifestyles that differ considerably from that of earlier generations. This process of change has taken place during the past two centuries and today colonizes growing parts of the world's cultures. Sociologists describe the process of modernization by four aspects:[19]

- Tradition loses its normative importance. What is new is normative, not that which has been. The human beings get their identity through what they have achieved in history, not through the position to which they were born. Action, development, and progress are the main words in the myth of modernity.

- "Decontextualization" (Anthony Giddens) and mobility are further distinctive features so that the importance of being deeply-rooted locally has diminished in favour of functional adaptation to the constantly changing constellations and demands of work and markets of merchandise and ideas. Nobody on the planet can assume that they can live in the same place during their entire lifetime. For most citizens of the world the right to stay with security is as hollowed out as the right to move freely.

- The replaceability of people and objects is a third feature. Goods, labour and people comprise a system of barter, which embraces the whole globe and reduces life worlds (Lebenswelten) more and more to objects. As it is not possible to biologically substitute life processes on one level with those of another level this trade system consumes irreplaceable natural resources. Products, biological material and individuals lose their liaison to specific local contexts. That which arises in a local situation is reduced to an object in a global barter market through the economic world system. In this way it loses its identity.

- "The colonialization of the life world through the system" (Jürgen Habermas) is a fourth feature. The system of monetary economy colonizes to an ever-increasing extent spheres of reality in the local life fellowships. The importance of ties to family, friends and relatives is played down in favour of relations tied to business contracts. The life fellowship is stripped of personal values. Vital forms of community no longer support society. Instead each community form constitutes a microcosmos of the general society. The constant production of conflicts is evidence of this mechanism and this process. Each community form is characterized in the modern state of things through conflict and breach: men against women, modern against traditional, poor against rich, etc. The concept of a social homogeneous fellowship has been weakened and been replaced by "the dialectic of enlightenment" (Max Horkheimer) which demands sacrifices for advancement.

Incarnation, Creation and Revelation

Apart from these reasons that are outside of church and theology there are also reasons for contextualization that emanate from an interpretation of Christianity's own tradition.[20]

The strongest reason lies in the mystery of incarnation. The distinctive feature of Christianity among other religions is the belief that God has become human, that the Creator has become flesh and blood among men and women. Revelation has thus taken place at a certain time, in a certain place and in a certain culture. God has through his/her Son in the shape of a human being become part of a certain sociocultural context. The universal God, Creator, has become particular: he is a male Jew, ideologically diffuse, wandering freely around in Palestine.

If Christian faith wants to preserve the continuity of its historical origins it needs somehow to preserve this particularity. After the revelation of God in Jesus the man, we cannot interpret Christian faith as a faith in a common, supernatural God. The distinctive features of the Christian image of God remain belief in a God, which meets us in a specific earthly and historical context with all the restrictions this signifies. This earthly historical belief cannot be reduced to metaphysics, a science of the supernatural.

The second reason is related to the theology of revelation. Because of the believer regarding all of reality as God's Creation and, therefore, in some sense sacred, there is no opposition between the divine and the worldly. Even if we may not place the Creation on a par with the Creator, the world and the history compose the space and the life within which the Creation is enacted. The belief in Creation also signifies that God reveals Him/Herself through Creation.

The Creation does not only have a passive and static function in the history of revelation. According to biblical and ancient church tradition, it is to a high degree a participating actor in the history of salvation. The earth, for example, acts together with God by keeping the dead until the time of resurrection or through engulfing evil people.[21] According to theologians researching ancient church history, the Creation actively announces God's will to humankind: climate change, for example, can make God's wrath visible over social injustice among humans.[22]

Believers may also understand the Creation as a theological sign system. It carries the mark of God (vestigia) and the sign of God (signatura).[23] We can interpret the revelation of God by reading the Bible like we can interpret it through studying the book of nature (liber naturae). It is in this that we can assume the seeds of modern natural sciences germinated.

If believers interpret the world in all its cultural and biological manifold and changeability as being divinely created and supported, then the mystery of incarnation also appears in a clearer light: "true God" meeting as "true man" the beings of the Creation in the middle of the space and time of Creation. The demand that theology ought to be contextual appears in the light of this as a most traditional thought.

A third reason for contextualization is that the view of revelation changed during the past century. Earlier approaches were that the revelation was an eternal truth about the essence of God which theology had to interpret with the help of an invariable, divinely given language. The second Vatican Council, for example, assumed that God offers him/herself to people in different places and that these people therefore ought to interpret their experiences out from their own conditions.

As a reflection of revelation, theology no longer becomes a matter for theologians with elite education with the privilege to construct a divine language aiming at the preaching of a number of true postulates of faith. Theology becomes a task for people in different contexts to interpret their experiences of the Creator and Liberator. It seems obvious that this view is in accordance with the biblical and older Christian traditions. The approach of contextual theology is not anything new. It rather expresses an aspiration for reconstruction and interpreting anew a theological self-understanding and method, which has been in use before the historical pattern which started to spread during the Renaissance and which still today modernizes the whole biosphere.

Summary

- Theology today ought to be contextual theology. By contextual we mean a Christian interpretation of life that is conscious of its circumstances. Contextual theology constitutes a reflection on experiences and expressions of the living and acting God in his/her multi-shaped revelations in the world. The understanding of the cultural manifold of the surrounding world constitutes a necessary prerequisite for developing strong and credible interpretations of Christianity.

- Research in Social and Cultural Studies challenges Religious Studies to reflect on the context of religious modes of expression and attach greater importance to them.

- The many Christians in the South convincingly criticize their siblings in the North for having disregarded the local and contextual character of their generalizing way of thinking. The criticism emphasizes that in this way, Christian belief has been able to legitimate an unjust Eurocentric colonial history lasting until now. The increasing self-confidence of local churches entails that this criticism is conveyed in more and more challenging forms. Contextual theology, therefore, is not only a matter for missionaries, but it also is a question of identity and survival for the European Christianity.

- Modernity has meant a quick transformation of the sociocultural ways of life. This has put theology partly in a hitherto unknown context and partly challenges it to become missiology again. New possibilities of communication and acting arise for Christians especially at a time when the old industrial modernity is "aging" (Ulrich Beck) and when the future of the modern way of life is uncertain.

- Several internal reasons speak in Christianity's own tradition for the task of contextualizing theology anew. The mystery of incarnation means that the Creator Him/Herself is part of a specific context and that the historical continuity of Christianity is preserved through constantly asking how God meets us in specific contexts. Contextual theology is incarnation theology about the Son and inhabitation theology about the Holy Spirit who dwells in and around us.

- Contextual theology is Creation theology. The profane and the sacred are not in opposition to one another as the cultural and biological manifold of the world is created and preserved by God. Contextual theology is a theology for the sake of the world. It does not legitimate an exclusive profession but aims at a reflection on experiences and encounters with the living God, who dwells in the Creation for the sake of its survival and renewal.

- Contextual theology shapes at the same time an old and new approach to theology's task of interpreting revelation. This task is not to interpret an unalterable content of faith with a divinely given language but to interpret individual's or group's experiences of the Creator and Liberator in certain places, in certain situations and at certain times. The contextualization of theology is an inevitable challenge to the whole interpretation of Christianity.

Notes

[1] On the term "contextual theology" and its history cf. Bosch, pp. 420–432.

[2] Coe.

[3] Cf. Boff, pp. 3–6.

[4] Cone, pp. 117–118, Frostin (1988), pp. 100–103, 176–177.

[5] Cf. Persson, who characterizes the task of theology in the title of his book as "To Interpret God Today" (Att tolka Gud idag).

[6] On the terms "liberation theology" and "contextual theology" see Bergmann (1995a), p. 464. Cf. also Bevans, pp. 18–19., who points out three criteria for "orthodoxy" (in accordance with J. de Mesas/L. Wostyn, in: Doing Theology: Basic Realities and Processes, Manila 1982.), and Schreiter's five criteria for an authentic local theology.

[7] Frostin (1992), p. 129.

[8] Schreiter, 6, pp. 20–21.

[9] Nolan, p. 12. Cf. Tanner, p. 92, who makes clear how this also is true for academic theology.

[10] Nolan, p. 18.

[11] Bevans, p. 5, differs between "external" and "internal" facts. His distinction seems not to make sense because of the historical problem of differing between church and society.

[12] See for example Moltmann, pp. 56–58.

[13] Tracy (1985), p. 36. A critical investigation of the history and potential of correlation theology cf. Bergmann (1995a), pp. 359-365. Cf. also Jeanrond, p. 174.

[14] Berger/Luckmann, p. 3 and p. 20.

[15] Cf. for example Rorty (1992), pp. 143–145, and his criticism of epistemology and the philosophy of "mentality".

[16] Cf. Foucault, pp. 10–14, and his criticism of the "will to truth" as a

discursive "system of exclusion".

[17]Cf. Hallencreutz, pp. 1–10. Also the Old Church in the patristic age should be, with Hallencreutz, p. 9, understood as a "church for and in the Third World".

[18]Merchant, pp. 2–3, pp. 261–270.

[19]These four points are a compressed result of my readings of Giddens', Beck's and Habermas' sociological studies.

[20]Beyond these reasons Bevans, p. 6, points out two further reasons, i.e. the fact that older theological methods obviously have been oppressive and that the local churches' self-reliance and consciousness has grown in the South.

[21]Cf. Moltmann-Wendel, pp. 412–413.

[22]Gregory of Nazianz, Oratio 16.5.

[23]Paracelsus develops a special doctrine of signs in order to interpret the signs of Creation and Jakob Böhme develops in accordance with Paracelsus a physiognomic semiotics of nature and a doctrine of nature's language. On the historical relationship between the Christian doctrine of signs and the hermetic tradition cf. H. Böhme, pp. 22–25, and G. B'ohme, pp. 124–129. On Jakob Böhme's view of nature cf. G. Böhme, pp. 129–137.

GECECEG

Gender
Economics
Class
Ethnicity
Culture
Ecolology
Geography

Chapter 2

Place and Perspective

The second chapter treats two questions:

- Which dimensions in the context are of importance for shaping theology?

- What approaches are being used in contextual theology?

Different Dimensions in the Context

Which factors in the surrounding world are of importance for theology?

When the Ecumenical Association of Third World Theologians (EATWOT) was founded in 1976 in Dar es Saalam, the delegates formulated six dimensions for understanding the conflict in world society. These six dimensions state the criteria for polarization between different groups of people:

- Economically, the rich differ from the poor.

- Class-wise, the owners of capital differ from the workers.

- Geographically, North differs from South.

- *Gender*
  Between the sexes, man differs from woman.

- Ethnically, for example, whites differ from blacks.

- Culturally, rulers differ from groups of people being ruled.[1]

I would like to add a seventh dimension, which ecologically differs between humans and other organisms. There is a conflict between the

[handwritten margin note:] Gender Economics Class ethnicity Ethnic Ecology Geography

exploitation of nature, the interests of society in the North and the survival interests of natural communities. We can, therefore, differentiate between exploiters and victims in cultural ecosystems.[2] Both humans and other organisms can sometimes be victims of the same cultural ecological violence.

By analyzing a context, we may likewise combine some of the EATWOT conference's six dimensions in the sphere of contacts between people. A poor black woman in the South may be part of the capital-weak class and the culture of the ruled. In the same South, a rich woman can be capital-strong and still be part of the ruled people. In the ecological sphere, pollution in the South may be of another kind than in the North. Poor and ruled indigenous people relate to the environment in another way than a globally ruling and rich group of eco-farmers in the North. Rich men in the South can act as economically unjust as rich women in the North.

The seven dimensions are significant for theology as well. They are given in each context and interact with the shaping of the Christian interpretation of life. We may naturally object that we do not need to take this into consideration to be able to talk about God.

Do we have to talk about the economic injustice and the battle between sexes when we talk about God? Is this just like changing Christian belief in God into an ideology by tying it to these seven perspectives on conflict? Do we give ourselves priority over God?

Such a criticism misses the point. The critic assumes that the origin of Christian theology is essentially different from the origin of an ideology. Roughly put: ideology is construed as something created while theology is construed as something non-created and divine.

The contextual theologian, on the other hand, assumes that each reflection interacts with the situation within which it arises. Theology is both the labour of man and woman and a participation in the mystery of revelation. Reflection on the view of humankind and society is embedded in the same conditions as reflection on God's image.

This does not mean that we reduce the interpretation of Christianity to an "-ism", an existentialism, Marxism or biologism. The main task of theology is not "to let God as God be heard again".[3] Through the words of the Niceano-Constantinopolitan confession, theology's task is to reflect on God's "economy" (Greek for history of salvation) as "true God and true human".

Contextual theology, therefore, rejects both an inclusive monotheism and an exclusively Christocentric confessionalism. God is not only everyone's God generally or the believer's Jesus especially. Contextual theology interprets God's actions as creative and liberating.

Theology and Ideology

The word ideology has struck a negative note in recent years and some people assert that all utopias and ideologies are at death's door after the fall of the Soviet Empire. The thesis of ideology's death is part of a neo-liberal criticism of society and religion which forwards the opinion that the comprehensive system of norms and religion ought to be understood as straight-jackets for the freedom of the individual. At last the individual can fulfil himself or herself on the free market and in the arena of competition. The categorical postmodernist uses the work ideology in the meaning of "the way of thinking and norm system which limits the space of action of the individual".

My definition of ideology joins the current definition and refers to the extensive system of norms and thought regulating communicative action and relations to nature by the main figures of society in a larger region.

It seems justified to ask if there is a strong need for new life-promoting ideologies in the situation of a growing transformation of forms in the older sets of values. The question is if declaring ideology dead enforces the dissipation of these sets of values rather than revitalizing the construction of new sets of values.

Contextual theology therefore includes a positive view of ideology's function in the process of society. Political theology, especially that which arose in Europe during the 1960s, asserted that the role of theology was to contribute to the growth of a life-promoting interpretation with political implications. Its hermeneutic principle was the "question of an authentic life for all people".[4]

The critic who says that ideology is one thing and theology is another, disregards this constructive intention. The function of theology is to "think God" (Dorothee Sölle) in such a way that it promotes everybody's life in a fellowship of nature and society. It is the specific and unique situation in which God meets us here today which is the focus of the incarnation-oriented contextual theology and not human experience and God generally.

It is evident that such a theology necessarily also brings social and political consequences. As critics, we cannot misinterpret the social and political importance as if they were the criteria for the appreciation of a good or bad interpretation of Christian faith. Theology's anchorage in the context and the relevance of theology for that context is one of several criteria and not the only one. The criteria of relevance need to be balanced by the criteria of identity, tradition and experience.

The social relevance of theology appears in the dialogue around the assessment of different ideologies. In relation to other ideological points of view, a Christian interpretation of what is emancipating or not in the societal process, could be precisely because of the question of God, both constructive and critical.

The abolition of the South African apartheid system, for instance, is not the same in itself as the propagation of God's kingdom even if we could interpret the repeal of the racial laws as a consequence of the liberating acts of the Lord. Theology will also in the new South Africa win a new and different function in the criticism of ideology even if the churches today are having difficulties in expanding their constructive role in a new situation. (As was the case with the churches in the old German Democratic Republic).

There is a tension between the Latin American theology of base communities with its focus on the people's economic liberation from northern superiority and the focus of South African theology on building up a strong democracy. This tension dates from the abolition of the apartheid system, and its importance should not be over-interpreted. In both regions, the theologians' reflection takes place in a close interaction with the ideological interpretations of society. They try to contribute critically and constructively to a structural view of society for everyone.

We should not misinterpret this as an attempt to render the fact that the interpretation of God in these different situations turns out differently relative to the Gospel. The differences and the similarities are, on the contrary, a sign that the same God acts in a liberating way in different places.

The suspicion of rendering relative to the Gospel was conveyed by the Vatican's Faith Congregation to the Latin American liberation theologians. The theologians were interrogated in Rome, a ban on speech and publishing was promulgated and a large number of intellectuals of the poor, as well as those bishops, who had committed themselves, were banned. The executioners in the secret services of dictatorships interpreted the controversy of faith, which the leading offices in Rome had unchained, as a carte blanche for torture and the execution of outspoken Christians.

Apart from the unscrupulousness of ignoring the moral aspect of the question, it was from the academic point of view embarrassing for the Faith Congregation that one did not even endeavour to understand the content of the criticized theology.

The theology of liberation departs from the fact that each citizen of the world independently of his or her goodwill lives in a field of suspense, which is characterized by the world's conflicts. Even human thinking and behaviour in different social scales is influenced by the dialectic of conflict. The theology of liberation quite simply departs from an existing social need of liberation from oppression. We may express it in the words of the prayer: deliver us from evil. This does not, in its turn, mean that all of reality constitutes a conflict. It means that the knowledge of conflict is unavoidable if we wish to understand human conditions and the apparition of God today.

Contextual theologians are of the opinion that no theologian of to-day can pass by the fact that the conflict between different groups of people is ongoing without losing its credibility. It is necessary not to close our eyes to the disastrous consequences of conflict. Furthermore, we must not close our eyes to its structural duration, inherent autonomy and idolatry.

If the theologian is to interpret the revelations and acts of our Lord in this world, then the decisive question arises how this God behaves towards the seven dimensions in the conflict in today's Creation. This is the question, which indicates the focus of contextual theology's perspective.

Since the time when Friedrich Nietzsche published his works, we know that each piece of knowledge and its rendering – description is perspectivistic and that knowledge which claims to describe uniform and objective truths a priori cannot be true.[5]

The choice of perspective and the elucidation of criteria and reasons that govern this choice are, therefore, necessary links in each scientific work on knowledge. Contextual theology satisfies these requirements through developing interpretation of different phenomena in reality whilst being aware of the perspective of knowledge.

While the theology of eternity was based upon the assumption of the existence somewhere of eternal truths which were laid down by God during the Creation and which the theologian sought and found, the contextual theologian seeks the manifold and element of surprise in Creation. Through the theology of eternity, recognition was elevated to principle in the static sphere, whilst contextualism uses the method of curiosity in an open changeable sphere. Scientifically theology does not strive exclusively for safe prognoses, but it is both looking backwards reflexively and transcending the perspective. This means it is open to the interpretation of the unexpected, the new and surprising.

The list of the above-mentioned seven dimensions in the global conflict and the contextual set of methods, help the theologian to localize himself or herself in the global field of tension. These dimensions may also be used to answer the question of theology's subject-matter: Who is the theologian? Is it a man or woman; financially strong or weak; over- or under-developed, modernized or half-modernized; white, yellow or black; powerful or powerless; a nature exploiter or a conservationist?

Theology for the World

The contextual theologian perceives his or her task as a service to the world for the world's sake and, therefore, presents himself/herself in a worldly manner before expounding his/her theological interpretations. For the sake of the whole, the theologian becomes involved in a modern world system, which constantly forces distinctions and divisions between the living.

The analysis of conflicts clearly shows the effect of context upon theology. We may not, however, confuse the conflict with the dimensions which helped us understand it. The differences between the sexes, for example, do not necessarily have to be filled with conflict to affect our perception and ways of thinking. The construction of the gender is less conflict-filled in Scandinavia than it is by the Mediterranean even though there are inequalities between the sexes in both regions. The perspective on the sex and gender interacts with the image of God in both regions in spite of geographical differences.

In reality we may state that different degrees of intensity in the conflict is a socially important factor for theology. As an example a church leader in an affluent northern European community has different experience with capital investors than his colleague in West Africa. A catholic cotton grower in Columbia has other experience with the World Bank than an evangelical leader of a computer business in China. The cultural violence against the ecosystem is of another kind in the Sahara than in northern Sweden. The prostitute in the Philippines meets the conflicts of sexes in Manila in another way than the female Member of Parliament in Stockholm.

Further social and cultural factors that are of great importance for the individual's understanding of reality are generation affiliation, educational level and place. Sociologists have shown how the fragmentation in the individual's understanding of reality accelerates in modern society. Generations differ greatly in their pattern of thought and behaviour and they change in time with shorter intervals. Already a 17-year-old can feel outside the younger teenager's view of values.

The high differentiation of educational levels, which slowly but surely is spreading also in developing countries, results in the formation of social layers in which the "stairs of knowledge" become higher with an increasing amount of steps. The climbing of this labyrinth of stairs makes the relation between qualifications through knowledge and the application more fragile and risky. In the lower part of the stairs the risks of being excluded increase, but also in the upper part of the stairs the feeling of powerlessness threatens as highly specialized fields of knowledge may quickly become redundant or obsolete.

The Significance of Urbanization

The place as a site for settlement and interaction influences to a great extent the individual's possibilities for choice of action. The pace of urbanization grows at the same rate in spite of material conditions in the larger cities appearing to be inferior to those of the countryside for many people in the North and South.

The highly differentiated pattern of behaviour offers a close to infinite choice of possibilities and opportunities. An individual staying outside of the city limits misses a lot and easily loses chances of success in the power game. Those who do not want to move to the centre, may be switched out of the network by those who manage the tools for guiding the flow of information and money at these centres. At the beginning of the 21st century, what is the centre is no longer decided by the urban planners in a metropolis but by the agents of the financial and technical-industrial markets.

The process of development in urban planning for the future has in spite of a large number of social and legal rules long since made itself independent. In the late modern industrial society, the evolution of the city no longer follows the human laws of growth/expansion. The space of the urban way of life has become unreal.[6]

The city lives its own life, and he or she who enters it may either drown in its flow of possibilities or advance to a position with at least some power over others. The city's power of attraction seems almost magical. It reminds us of the holy sites of past times.

The function that individuals and groups have in the city's life form is, as yet, a totally non-investigated factor of importance for theology. However, it is obvious that the image of God and encounters with God in "the secular city" (Harvey Cox) create totally unknown perspectives and problems for Christian faith.

In this context, a challenge to future academic, contextual theology would be investigating how the urban life form of the metropolis interacts with the image of God and how the experiences of the conflict and God's acts of troubleshooting are interpreted in different types of metropolis theology. The question is how the physical and social mental imaging of a built inner space and an outer city environment affects the experience of God and our thinking.[7]

Even if the importance of the place for thinking has long since been overshadowed, we cannot exaggerate its importance.[8] It is obvious that the creation of space of a place where people act communicatively with each other and the geographical position of the place within a surrounding townscape or landscape, qualitatively influences our patterns of perception, thought and action.

It is this old insight which, during different eras, led to human understanding and caring for sacred places where they have built holy temples and churches.[9] Sacred spaces are not only places where humans have expressed their views of life and images of God. They also have a power to influence perception and behaviour in other places.

The Profane is the Sacred Space

The sacred space is delimited physically but not mentally from the profane space. The signification of the holy also gives meaning to the profane space. Richard Sennett, has shown how the holy places and places for fellowship and compassion during medieval times contrast with the market's places for competition, egoism and violence.[10]

The place has an aesthetic importance-shaping potential, which works independently whether it is understood as holy or as profane. In pastoral, contextual theology we try to integrate different meanings of sacred and profane spaces.

Each place in Creation is understood as a possible place for revelation. Each place is construed as a possible agent for cooperation with the liberating God. The Holy Spirit not only gives life to a creature in a place but also animates the space. It is especially the places which are seen as profane in a culture that attract the interest of contextual theologians.

A study of the early history of Christianity shows that the thought of the profane place's revaluation runs like a common thread through the Gospels. The lowly manger for the cattle became the place of the birth of God; the hill of skulls, Golgata, near the refuse tip in the holy city became the place of His death. The grave where they laid His body was borrowed from the rich.

The human God of the Gospels unlike the God of the Hebrews and the gods of the Greeks was surprisingly restless and placeless. He was either on a pilgrimage or was roaming about, or temporarily stayed with someone, or he was simply a down-and-out. The poor and badly reputed northern part of the country was unexpectedly the starting point for the missionary's journey to the centre of power. The inhabitants of Jerusalem do not seem to have digested the assertion of destroying and rebuilding the walls of the most holy building even today.

It does not seem to become calmer and more place-bound with the Holy Spirit either. According to the evangelist, she blows where she wants and the metaphors air and wind which characterize her apparition choose the least place-bound of nature's four elements. This is in spite of the local metaphor fire that is regularly being used.

Looking at the first century of Christianity in a topographic perspective, a very mobile and dynamic pattern appears where the mobility seems to be superior to the binding to a place. At the same time, the signification of a large number of profane and sacred places are "reloaded" with totally new import.

While the sites of the first and second century are associated with courses of events and acts, the third century is characterized by a long-term stabilizing of the religious map in the context of time. Christian places of meeting arise not only where needed but where we began to build churches.[11] Following this period, we see two kinds of topographic strategies for the propagation of Christian faith. On the one hand, churches are being built at the former sacred places and on the other, something which we might call a religious map is being established across the open landscape.

In the wilderness, altars are put up and together with litanies consecrated to martyrs. Ascetics settle in deserts and other non-cultivated regions. Monastic communities settle on mountaintops that were difficult to reach. Pilgrimages between places in memory of important religious events colonize the land and create a new net between points of revelation history.

Sennett shows how the Christian conception of the body and especially the importance of the suffering of Christ have influenced medieval city formation. Christian places have offered refuge for compassion and fellowship in the context of developing capitalization and individualization of the (pre)modern society.[12]

The growth of Christianity in the Palestine and later in the whole Mediterranean region, in other words, redraws the maps of the sacral and profane landscape in a very radical way. An inventory of the building of churches in the world shows that this process is still ongoing with even greater intensity and extent in Africa and Asia.

The religious landscape of Christian history and the modern city's differentiated map are of great importance for the shaping of theology. An interpretation of the connection between city architectonic, culture geographical, and culture anthropological perspectives on the development of the interpretation of Christianity, would with all certainty give interesting and unexpected insights on the possibilities for contextual theology in the city- and landscape.

We can now summarize the different factors for the understanding of the context and demand that the contextual theologian is well versed in the theory and formation of concepts in the cultural and social sciences. While the pastoral theology ought to be well integrated with the different local agents' understanding of reality, the contextual theology in the academic sphere is shaped in a strong awareness of interdisciplinary discourse.

It is not necessary for the theologian to master all the methods that may elucidate the factors relevant for the interpretation of Christianity and the organization of the church. It is, however, necessary to organize an interdisciplinary problem-oriented distribution of work.

It is not necessary either that each pastoral or academic attempt is up to date with the latest findings. A reasonable demand is that the proposals of contextual theology do not contradict known insights into the social and cultural sciences.

A more ambitious demand is that the educational system of academic theology offers knowledge about the importance of religion for the societal and culture-shaping process. A definition of borders which are too acutely drawn between the social sciences and humanities on the one hand and religious science on the other precludes the growth of such knowledge. The same is true for the conflict between representatives of the mutually excluding perspectives of religion history and systematic theology.

Considering the urgent pastoral challenge to a new interpretation of the Christian image of God, knowledge of the urban way of life stands out as an important tool for the interpretation of Christianity in northern Europe. Considering the accelerating disintegration of the cultural and biological manifold, a productive approach is a dialogue with human ecology and its knowledge of the interaction between modernity, subject and the environment as well as the function of religion in the criticism of civilization.

While theology found its early partner in discussions and collaboration with philosophy and later sociology, contextual theology develops the dialogue and co-operation with the cultural sciences. Theology ought to develop active contact with the parts of the natural sciences and technology, which are oriented towards humans and environmental protection rather than towards the interest of financial accumulation.[13] In other words, no scientific and pastoral co-operation project, which aims at an increased understanding of the context, ought to be foreign to the contextual theologian.

Different Ways of Approaching Contextual Theology

What approaches are being used in contextual theology?

Since I understand theology as a course of events where individuals and groups actively express and reflect on their own and other's experiences with the living and acting God, it would be presumptuous to try to summarize and describe all the forms of expression of this process in a single book.

The road from the act of God to the experience of God and from there to a communicative expression or a rite, and further to a verbal or figurative description of experiences may be long and tricky. The theologian who only devotes himself/herself to the studying of texts easily ignores the complexity, which distinguishes the flow between experience, expression and reflection in a Christian interpretation.

The method of text interpretation, therefore, needs to be extended and supplemented by methods which enable us to understand the processes underlying the origin of the texts. Systematic theology also needs to widen the horizons of its interpreted objects from the texts to pictures, rites, conversations and the everyday course of events. This extension is especially important considering that the late modern culture increasingly reduces the importance of a text in favour of non-linguistic media like music, pictures and drama. At the same time, many people understand the transmission of linguistic messages as superior in comparison with the written text. This does not mean, though, that it really is easier to express oneself and be understood over the telephone than by letter.

There are several courses of action to describe the manifold of different ways of working in theology. In the following I combine a conventional systematic method with an anthropological definition of religion.

Systematically I will interpret some texts where the authors themselves claim to represent contextual theology. Anthropologically I ask where and how Christians express faith in the "God in function". A dependable answer to the first question is possible thanks to the international book- and library system. The answer to the second question can only be hinted at due to the lack of extensive work on the source material.

Contextual Interpretation of Life on Five Continents

Contextual theology is a Christian interpretation, which is shaped in consciousness of the context. Contextual theologies are different interpretations of life, which are distinguished through a common view of the method of theology.

In a geographical perspective we may note that contextual theologies in this meaning have grown up on all the continents of the globe since the demand for the contextualization was formulated in 1973.

This does not mean that consciousness of the social and cultural situation did not emerge until 1973. It simply means that Christians in different regions have developed the concept formation of the word "context" in relation to the notion "theology" and granted it surprisingly quick and geographically all-encompassing diffusion between 1973 and 1990.

From the year 1989 we find the notion "contextual theology" in the odd dictionary. It is the creation of a precise lexiographic definition, which makes a word into a communicatively normative and analytical notion.[14]

As this text is being written, it is still a question addressed by handbooks or manuals in Religious and Mission Studies. Considering the accelerating concept formation in other scientific fields, i.e. social anthropology and the history of art, we may expect a continued increasing spread of the concept's use and its language and thought-structuring importance.[15]

From the start, the use of the term contextual theology has been intensive in South Africa and in Asia. On the other hand, theologians in Latin America preferred to develop the term "liberation theology" as their comprehensive main concept.

The Latin American liberation theology may be designated as a contextual theology without hesitation because the base communities and the theologians shape it in an indissoluble integration with a political situation of conflict and thereby independently make use of sociological theories.

In South Africa the Institute of Contextual Theology was founded early in Johannesburg. It has filled a very important function for the organizing of the ecclesiastical anti-apartheid movement. The institute in Johannesburg has also been the driving force and the communicative space within which the South African Christians of different confessions have carried through the important Kairos process.[16]

While in South Africa and Latin America, theology has mainly been oriented towards the political and socio-economic dimensions of the context, in other parts of Africa and Asia, more weight has been attached to the cultural dimension of the context. The Minjung theology focuses on the people's collective suffering and uses to a greater extent the Asiatic forms of culture and religion to interpret the wounded people's painful life context.

The independent African churches in, for instance, Zimbabwe emphasize the cultural and ecological dimension. They develop a very independent synthesis between traditions in the African traditional religion and the charismatic theology in the North. This synthesis leads to endowing the Christian interpretation of life an ethical meaning in terms of environmental control and the fight against the spreading desert in Zimbabwe.[17]

In the Middle East, contextual theology is still in a weak position. The religious map in the Middle East presents a very complex picture since political interests from the west and the north, as well as the missionary interests have been very strong in this region.

Christians, who follow contextual theology, are found today mainly among the Palestinian believers, where the struggle against occupation, the intifada, during most of the 1980s has functioned as a catalyst to increase the church's and theology's consciousness of the importance of the context.[18]   Attempts at a Jewish theology of liberation exist even if these originally were developed in the United States.[19] It seems natural in the Palestine to have mainly attached significance to the political and social aspects of the context and also to have emphasized the intercultural and interreligious aspects.

We find an ambiguous interest in contextual theology in the areas dominated by the Eastern Church's orthodox movements of faith. While the orthodox theologians in the Western hemisphere are intensively interested in contextual methodology, church leaders in the older principal areas of Orthodoxy construe this as a modern invention. While some in the orthodox "family" of the ecumenical movement work out contextual interpretations of life and faith, others seem to be more negative.[20]

It is interesting that, for instance, Aram I, the catholicos of the Armenian Apostolic Church, who is one of the chairmen in the World Council of Churches, in a statement before the mission conference in

1996 views the culture as a "tool" with "temporary value". He contrasts this view of culture against Judaism, Islam and Hinduism for which, according to Aram I, "the original culture is a holy model for the meeting with the last judgement".[21]

We may wonder if with such a point of view the orthodox creed is threatened by a too exclusive instrumentalization of the culture. The Byzantine-influenced Orthodoxy probably has a solid work programme ahead if it wants to take part in contextualizing theology.

My opinion is that the orthodox intellectuals, who had to emigrate from Russia in the beginning of the century after the revolution, are the normative people. Immigrating and emigrating theologians like Sergej Boulgakov and Paul Evdokimov have laid a good foundation for future orthodox contributions to contextual theology through their successful transformation of the orthodox faith to new surroundings.

In Australia we find contextual theologians partly among the immigrated English-speaking inhabitants, whom we can compare with theologians in North America and Europe, and partly among the original inhabitants, the Aborigines. In the later group I have not noticed any use of notions even if on the missions and in the reservations great ability is found to integrate Aborigine and Christian traditions and let this synthetic worldview regulate behaviour.[22]

The Christians in the Yabarrah reservation, for example, interpret the cultural encounter between the aboriginal and the immigrated population in a very original way. During the 1980s, we can, therefore, discern the growth of a different and earlier unknown synthesis of a partly Christian, charismatic and liberal theological view of life and a partly aboriginal view of life. This theology creates such considerable cultural self-confidence, that the Christians in Yabarrah today see themselves as missionaries in relation to the Westerners who they feel have lost contact with the springs of spirituality. In Chapter 6 about the importance of art for theology, we will meet a visual expression of how the aboriginal Christian view of life is capable of illuminating the situation and tradition of Creation.

In North America and in Europe primary groups, clerics and academic theologians are developing different approaches to contextual theology. For this process, important communicative spaces are offered by the ecumenical movement as well as by the parishes. Here Christians and members of other popular movements are able to meet each other to discuss important social problems, like feminist-, environment-, peace- and solidarity-issues. A third space sometimes arises in academic activities where theologians of many different scientific, philosophical and confessional backgrounds treat important social problems.

In Europe during the 1960s, "political theology" developed and within it great attention was paid to the social political dimension under the aspect of justice. During the 1970s, issues like the treatment of women, environment and peace were most in the foreground, and during the next decade it was the agenda of global economics that aroused the most interest. The cultural dimension of the context was beginning to be paid attention to as well. In spite of the material resources for the development of contextual forms of expression being much larger in the North than in the South it seems that the creativity in the poor nations is greater than in the rich nations. In the North we are only just able to discern an institutionalization of contextual theology on a small scale while on the long-term stable organizations have been built up in, for example, Costa Rica and South Africa.

In 1991, in the Nordic countries, academically active theologians founded in 1991 the network for researchers in contextual theology, and in the same year came the initiative to found the association the Institute for Contextual Theology in Lund, Sweden. In northern Norway the non-conformist theologian Roald E. Kristiansen pleads for a geographically identified "theology of northern Norway".[23] In several countries in Europe there are today a number of freestanding organizations and foundations, which apply a contextual perspective and we may expect that the many, small theological interpretations of life in a near future may be visible and homogeneous. In this way it may become important for the ecumenical movement. The historically important European Church Meeting in Basel in 1989 gave a sure sign of developments to come.

Kairos Theology

An important driving force for the development for contextual theology in Europe and in the United States is the Kairos movement. "Kairos" is a Greek word for time. In the New Testament it indicates a particular time that makes demands. It is a time of crisis but also a time of departure. The time of challenge and choice of road had come with Christ according to the Gospel. It was time and belief in the Gospel demanded conversion in thought and way of life. One could say that kairos is the main word for an eschatology, that is an interpretation of Christianity which especially places the future in the centre. (The Greek word "eskaton" means the space of the last time).

During the 1970s and 1980s the interest in eschatology returned to theology. In South Africa, the first so-called kairos-process was initiated which led to a clear Christian position in the racial oppression. Then in turn came the Central American Christians who created theology in small groups with the same methodology. The analysis of society was combined with Bible reading and interpretation of faith.

Similar processes of reflection were gradually started also in Europe and in the United States. A Kairos document was published by a group in Lund, Sweden, in 1989. At the ecumenical meeting "For the sake of life" which was held in 1992 in Lund, a women's Kairos process was begun.

In 1989 all European churches gathered for the concilium in Basel. They were successful in uniting around a number of clear answers to the challenges represented by the threats to survival. During the ongoing church meeting, around 30 participants gathered to promise each other to bring the process from words to action. At the JPIC world meeting in Seoul in 1990, the representatives of groups for justice from all continents decided to let the activities culminate during the year 1992. The "Kairos Europe" network was founded in May 1990 with approximately 120 groups. In 1995 around 500 groups were affiliated.

During Pentecost 1992, 750 delegates from Kairos Europe assembled at a meeting in Strasbourg. The participants represented groups, which organize the victims and groups, which were loyal to these. A delegation participated from Sweden representing Christian homosexuals, the Sami, women, primary groups, small-scale farmers, the unemployed, the Christian Peace Movement, the churches' development forum and two members of Parliament. The five themes of the meeting, (agriculture, living and environment, work, free settlement, cultural identity), composed important priorities in assessing the problematic situation for the victims in Europe.

The Kairos Europe movement stands out among the people's movements through its double strategy. On the one hand, it is desirable to contribute to a long-term build-up of power against the economistic world system. Those that were victimized should organize themselves and find forms of resistance and construction of alternatives. On the other hand, one looks for such points where groups of victims and groups in solidarity could be politically active with the purpose of changing the conditions of future development.

In relation to the Christian churches, the Kairos movement formulates a number of challenging problems. Are the churches ready to side with those reduced to silence? Are they willing to act as loyal spokesmen for those victimized by economic repression? How is a church administration, which itself puts most of its capital into the prevailing monetary system, able to credibly advocate and practise economic conversion?

The double strategy of the Kairos movement challenges the churches to regional and international expansion of the welfare worker's responsibilities in combination with a sociological and global economic analysis. It further demands that churches and parishes mix into the current daily political debate without having to face arguments that faith and politics do not blend. This is in accordance with the tradition of Christian social ethics of love for the poor.

In their analysis of the South African Church's Kairos in the apartheid society, Christians showed in 1985 that there were three possible attitudes for the churches to take towards an unjust system:

- state theology (an authorization of the prevailing power constellation),

- church theology (supposed neutrality in the conflict, not for the sake of the weak but for the sake of all and above all for one's own sake),

- prophetic theology (criticism of the injustice on the victim's premises in the light of biblical and Christian tradition).

This partitioning into three is also valid for the contribution by the Kairos movement to the social understanding of a global power, which is governed by money adoration. If liberation theologically means liberation from idolatry, then neither economic theology, which authorizes the governing powers nor a putatively neutral and liberal theology, preserving the status quo, is possible. Only a prophetic and eschathologic theology may, according to the Kairos movement, understand the acting God's encounter with the people He/She created.[24]

Feminist Theology

Looking at the growth of contextual theology in a perspective of gender theory we notice two tendencies.[25] First, the female perspective develops in a large number of social spheres and sciences. The women's movement grows with a critical and constructive force for the shaping of society. Feminist theology mirrors and contributes to this process. Thanks to the extensive and quick spread of women's perspective to many different regions in the world, women's theology differentiates as well in a very large number of points of view which often converge but at times also confront each other.

The second tendency is the lack of reflection upon the sex and gender in contextual theology in the South between the 1970s and 1980s. It was later when the theologians in the South perceived the social injustice to the gender on their own horizon. The ecumenical movement's women's decade has been a successful project where the member churches have tried spreading and deepening the consciousness of the context's gender-social aspects with Christians in different parts of the world. The effects of this increased consciousness is apparent in the Christian church's active and qualified contributions to the UN conferences on population problems in Cairo in 1994, on development questions in Copenhagen in 1994 and on women's questions in Peking in 1995, among others.

Asian Women's Theology

In the Korean theologian Chung Hyun Kyung's approach, we find an example of how contextual theology seeks a union of several perspectives on the context. She was born 1956 in Korea and participated early on as youth representative to the World Council of Churches' general assembly. In 1991 she attracted great attention at the World Council of Churches' general assembly in Canberra when she made use of shaman rites and dances to raise the spirits' ancestors and, at the same time, lectured on her perspective of the Holy Spirit's deeds in Christian tradition.

Chung's message was not really so controversial as regards content because she in good, socially ethical, and ecumenical spirit linked up to "the world agenda" (Uppsala 1968), that is, to questions regarding women, peace and environment. The orthodox delegates above all perceived her mixture of a religious Asian and Christian form of expression as provocative. Reading her lecture as text, though, the content seemed surprisingly uninfluenced by the Asian interpretation of reality. The form of her expression, on the other hand, contained more Asian elements.

In her book from 1990, "Struggle to be the Sun again", Chung Hyun Kyung develops the same view as in Canberra and presents her own theology as the "Asian women's theology".[26] Among many things she pleads shortly for a synthesis of the shaman and Christian religions.[27] Chung, who defended her doctoral thesis in the United States and works as a professor in Seoul, links up to the theology of liberation and accentuates the personal and political task of theology.

Her attempt is contextual in the sense that she forms the Christian interpretation of life in a very high awareness of partly the gender social and the social political and partly the religious cultural context in which her and the Asian women's theology will be relevant.

Chung wants to be the voice of the poor and she pleads for an "inductive, collective and inclusive method" for theology.[28] The dialogue with the suffering women is the basic experience to which she wants to listen and on which she will build her theological reflection.

I will not discuss how far we can view her attempts as authentic and consistent. We could however ask if Chung's generalizing interpretation of the Asian woman's reality does not leave too much unsaid. Furthermore, we may ask if she does not regard the prerequisites for her own academic theological activities in relation to the female forms of expression too uncritically. We may also wonder if Chung does not act too much in the global arena of communications rather than on the terms of her suffering sisters.

Methodically one may ask if the inclusiveness that she tries to attain is not rather a typically western way of approaching human reason. The question is if an individual theologian really can include all of Creation in her personal and particularly shaped interpretation of life.

Chung's theology leaves many questions unanswered. It is not distinguished by any special ability towards self-criticism. On the other hand, the Korean theologian's uncompromising will and ability to dare the synthesis between different points of view is interesting. In this way, her project expresses the contextualizing of theology, which takes the theological challenge to global communication seriously. This social and cultural change of communications system in the global society challenges the religious communities to create new forms of exchange between Christians in various countries and in different social groups.[29] In this context, the "phenomenon Chung Hyun Kyung" and the reactions to her acting are at least as important as her literary production.

Ecofeminist and Ecological Theology

Other approaches with several dimensions in contextual theology exist within the so-called ecofeminism which make up a qualified synthesis of environmental science and gender studies. Theologians like Sallie McFague, Grace Jantzen, Rosemary Radford Ruether, Anne Primavesi and Mary Grey have deepened the ecofeminist theology.

The North American philosopher Karen J. Warren develops an epistemological perspective of ecofeminist spirituality.[30] According to her, there are five important distinctive features in a patriarchal worldview.[31]

- Value hierarchical thinking where one thinks in categories of "up" (reasonable, strong and controlled = male) and "down" (feeling, bodily, passive and submissive = female).

- Dualism of values, where one thinks in the category either-or and puts different parts of reality in contrast to each other.

- The view of power as "power over" which aims at preserving the relations of control and subordination.

- The concept of privileges which aim at preserving "power-over relations" between those "up there" and those "down there".

- The logic of dominating, which constitutes an argumentative structure justifying the power and privileges of those "up there" in relation to those "down there" on the basis of the assumption that superiority justifies subordination.

Warren and many others consider that the same dualistic and hierarchic way of thinking and perception also steers the view of nature in the patriarchal view of the world. Ecofeminism asserts that sexism and "naturism" (the repression of nature) follow the same logic.

According to Warren, the patriarchate constitutes a "dysfunctional system", that is, a social system which norms are not clear, negotiable and consensual but are unchangeable, rigid and confused.[32] Such a system demands a high degree of control as opposed to open systems. It also brings with it a narrowing and blinding of the wide angles of the understanding of reality. Dysfunctional social systems breed powerlessness and helplessness among its citizens.

The ecofeminist spirituality offers a life promoting, personal empowering and collectively constructive challenge to the dysfunctional patriarchal society. Warren shows how women and nature, represented by animals, are brought together in accordance with the dualism of value in the same group. By likening women to animals, this expresses their inferiority in comparison to men even stronger The exploitation of the women is justified as a "naturalization".

Warren further shows how the patriarchal society comprises a big unmanageability and that it is exactly this, which contributes to its duration.

From her analysis, Warren draws the conclusion that the ecofeminist philosophy has to scrutinize the historical, social and economic, political and cultural conditions of patriarchal society. It cannot operate just like that with a simple notion of health. That which is deemed healthy in nature and in the family is too easily decided with the help of the hierarchical and dualistic value thinking.

The experience of the earth's and nature's different integrity and innate value makes up an important source for the ecofeminist experience and struggle. This experience offers a real possibility to step out of the patriarchal reality.

Warren's analysis is to the point in its interpretation of the gender-constructed injustice in the global system. Her analysis needs to be completed, though, with other interpretations of the state of society so that the perspective of women does not dominate "over" other perspectives of the context and so as to keep its sting.

Warren does not really offer a theological interpretation, although I find her reference to the non-patriarchal experience of nature very interesting. Both women and men may expand their horizons by recourse to nature and in this way correct their experiences and conceptualizations in the inter-human sphere.

The experience of nature is in itself an indispensable potential for the criticism of civilization and the tradition of ideas, only the romantic philosophy of nature has been capable of administering "the pound" in an adequate way and friends of nature are often charged with the epithet romantics. In my eyes they ought to take it as a badge of honour. Warren's attempt could favourably be realized as theology of the Creation and this is a project that has been started by, above all, Rosemary Radford Ruether.

In ecological theology, there are further attempts, which show a strong synthesis of different points of view in the history of salvation in nature and in society.

Theologians here regard nature not only as a life-less space for creation but they also seek the deeds of the Son and the Holy Spirit in Creation.

The German protestant theologian, Christian Link, talks about the "transparency of nature" and means that nature is a necessary condition for Creation.[33] In my pneumatological and trinitarian shaped ecological theology of liberation, I have accented the importance of manifold in the Holy Spirit's shapes of revelations.[34]

The biologist and theologian, Günter Altner, considers that nature and the process of evolution make visible a Creation under the cross, i.e. they reveal God's participation in the life and suffering process of Creation.[35]

Elisabeth Moltmann-Wendel shows that the thought of the earth's participation in no way is unknown in Christian tradition. The earth

in the Jewish and the Christian bible and in the treasure of psalms
has been perceived as an independent subject in co-operation with the
redeeming Creator.[36]

In my book, "Geist, der Natur befreit" (Spirit, liberating nature),
I have related how the growing ecological image of nature offers differentiated possibilities for a new interpretation of the Christian tradition
of God acting liberatingly in, with and through nature. In this book
I argue for a trinitarian shaping of an "ecological liberation theology"
and begin such a development by especially making use of the tradition
of the doctrine of the Spirit to focus on the significance of place.

Biblical Theology for Social Economic Justice

Another synthetic attempt is by Ulrich Duchrow who investigates the
history of ideas, economy, colonialism, and theology and the aspects
of this related to the growth of the global economic system. Duchrow
shapes the interpretation of biblical history and the Gospel's image of
God in a normative way which aims at overcoming the global system.
His theology comes into being in the context of the above-mentioned
European Kairos movement. Duchrow's books, therefore, may not be
compared with academic monographs as his texts are addressed at read-
ers who are both committed and knowledgeable of the subject. They
stand out through a different and more accurately aimed relevance for
agents in people's movements and churches.

At the centre of Duchrow's contextual theology is the question: "Is
there a way to justice after 500 years of plunder, oppression, accumulation and idolization of money?"[37]   To enable the churches and
people's movements to practically follow this road, Duchrow suggests
co-operation in three objects of action,[38]

- to curb the political and financial structures of power through
  prophecy and increased rights,

- to give regional models to transformed societies by developing
  functioning contrast societies in niches,

- to globally refuse cooperation with the life-destroying systems and
  build up local networks between groups of victims and those who
  are loyal.

Duchrow differs from other social theoreticians and theologians by
attaching an important function of explaining the current state of society to the historic process.

These insights, which the growth of the contextual attempts mirror, mean for the church, that it ought to seek a renewal of its identity in consciousness of the new social conditions. The situation of an increasing ethnic, religious, and cultural pluralism makes it impossible to present a picture of the faith of the church as the one and obviously universally applicable source of the whole of the social value and norm system. Contextual theology's differentiation of the image of God and related similarities and differences of gender, ethnicity, geography, ecology and world economics also challenge the different churches to develop a new social shape expressing and furthering openness for both differences and similarities, for nearness and distance. Especially problematic is here the structure and self-understanding of the large societies, which to a high degree rests on integration and mirroring of the history of homogeneous society. The challenge is about developing the identity of the church and religious fellowships as a "contrast society" (N. Lohfink) in accordance with the biblical traditions.[39]

Many contextual theologians are concerned with the current situation's interaction with experiences of God and they, therefore, sometimes oversee the fact that linguistic and cultural ways of thinking and forms of expression are handed over during a long space of time. Consequently, the historical perspective constitutes a necessary part of the context analysis. In the following chapter we will, therefore, especially go in-depth to the problem of handing-over.

Summary

We can summarize what is important for the understanding of the context in five points:

- The question if the context simultaneously contains the question of theology's subject and context: Who does theology? For whom and with whom is theology being done?

- Analysis of the context starts from, first, reality being impressed by conflict and it emphasizes the importance of polarization between people and between human beings and the environment. It starts from, second, modern society's pattern of differentiation and emphasizes the meaning of differences. We find an important factor in the signification of the place and the surrounding landscape.

Gender
Economics
Class
Ethnicity
Generation
Education
Culture
Ecology
Geograph
Place.

- The significance of context for theology is, in this way, under-standable with the help of the following ten social, cultural and ecological factors: geography / gender / ethnic affiliation / cultur-ally constructed power / class / economy / ecology / generation / education / place.

- These factors can again be divided into three groups:

  - factors in the physical surrounding world,

  - factors relating to the subject,

  - social and cultural factors.

- We can illustrate the significance of context for theology in a figure that grasps the Christian interpretation of life as seen from the revelation of God, which expresses itself as an interaction between all of these factors.

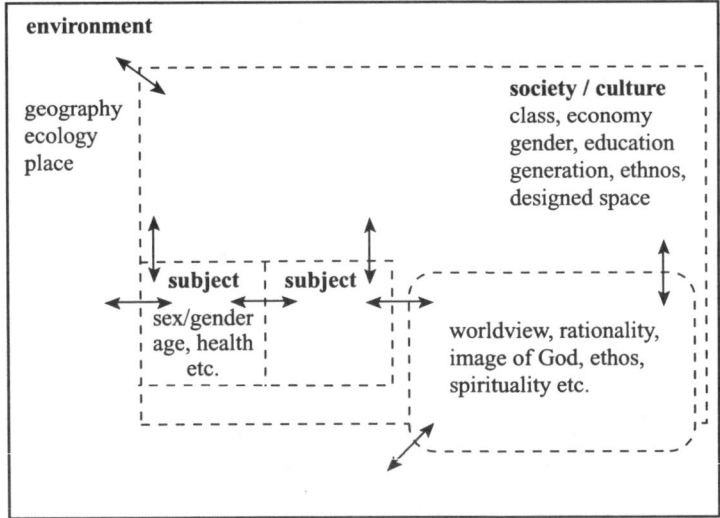

Figure 2.1: The Christian interpretation of life in the interaction of different factors in the context

- Even if the above-sketched overview of different geographically de-fined theologies form a narrow basis, we may note some tendencies in the history of contextual theology.

- The Christian interpretation of life is contextualized to an increasing extent in a growing number of places on all the five continents.

- In different circumstances, theologians attach varying significance to the different dimensions of the context. In certain countries the social and economic dimensions are illustrated, in others the cultural, and in other countries again the dimension of gender or the ecological dimension. Combinations between the different dimensions like, for example, in ecofeminism, occur in the analysis of text the more development and globalization progresses.

- The conflict on the one hand, between attempts in the women's, peace, and environmentally-oriented domains in the North and, on the other hand, the social and economic cultural attempts in the South, are slowly won over to the benefit of a collective view on the complex interaction of context with theology. From the 1980s, the number of theologians that unite several dimensions of their analysis of context is increasing. At the same time, the older single-question theologies are decreasing in importance.

- The process of communication between theologians in the third and fourth worlds and even in the first world is increasing in importance. In tune with the increasing number of Christians in the North that are interested in trying contextual methods, the significance of creative Christian interpretations of life increase in the South.

- The notion "contextual theology" contributes linguistically and intellectually to the integration of the many different theological expressions which can then form a manifold interpretation pattern of God's acts, of God in function today at home and over there. The younger contextual theology regards God's revelation and creation in a more complex and humble way, even though, in a perspective which as subjectively as the older attempts in liberation theology, it shares God's passion for the liberation of the suppressed.

Notes

[1]The criteria of the EATWOT-conference in: Frostin (1988), p. 8.

[2]Cf. Bergmann (1995a), p. 321

[3]Tracy (1994), p. 38.

[4]Sölle (1971), p. 77.

[5]On Nietzsche's understanding of the perspectivistic knowledge see Picht, p. 22–26.

[6]Scherpe, p. 8.

[7]Cf. Bergmann (1996b).

[8]On the significance of place for the the construction of identity see Relph, pp. 49–55.

[9]An extensive survey of the research on relations between Religious Studies and Geography is offered by Park.

[10]Sennett, p. 236.

[11]The late antique, Cappadocian patristic theologian Gregory of Nazianz offers the oldest written description of a Christian church building. Gregory tells us emphatically how his father Gregory the elder in the midst of the fourth century promoted the building and decoration of the eight-cornered church in Nazianz. The text is found in Oratio 18.39, and a reconstruction of the plan is offered in Bergmann (1995a), p. 419. The Christians inculturated their faith through this building in regard to the Eastern Byzantine architecture and to the classical theory of representation of the empire. Cf. Sennett, p. 179., who discusses why the Christian community later on builds time-durable constructions.

[12]Sennett, p. 231.

[13]Cf. Bergmann (1995b), p. 45, and Daly/Cobb, pp. 401-404.

[14]Regarding the meaning of the term see Schreiner.

[15]Cf. Irarrázaval.

[16]The result of the process is summarized in the document: "Kairos South

Africa".

[17]Daneel shows in his article how thoughts from Northern European Creation theology can be integrated into a synthesis of traditional African religion and the Independent churches' charismatic theology in order to contribute to environmental protection in Zimbabwe.

[18]A survey on the landscape of palestinian theology in the history of intifada is offered in the anthology edited by Ateek, Ellis and Radford Ruether.

[19]The North American theologian Marc H. Ellis develops his Jewish theology of liberation in a sharp settlement with the Jewish people's traumatic self-understanding in the light of the Holocaust.

[20]Limouris' anthology offers a survey on the ecumenical contributions of orthodox theology to an ecological Creation theology.

[21]Hela jorden, vol. 149, 5/1995, p. 24.

[22]Hume, pp. 260–261.

[23]Cf. Kristiansen, Ruus, pp. 21–45.

[24]Cf. Tergel, pp. 479–480, who shows how the history of the ecumenical movement from the 70's is profiled by the topic of social justice at the centre of its theology and ecclesiology.

[25]Ursula King offers an extensive survey in her "Introduction: Gender and the study of religion", pp. 1–38.

[26]Chung Hyun Kyung, p. 41.

[27]Chung Hyun Kyung, p. 130.

[28]Chung Hyun Kyung, p. 186.

[29]Cf. the General Assembly of the WCC in Canberra 1991 and its consensus on the challenge to an ethics for the media: Section II, Issue 4 "The Challenge of Communication for Liberation", Canberra, p. 85.

[30]Warren, p. 121.

[31]Warren, pp. 122–123.

[32]Warren, pp. 125–129.

[33]Link, pp. 176-184.

[34]Bergmann (1995a), p. 349.

[35]Altner, pp. 98–100.

[36]Moltmann-Wendel, pp. 419-420.

[37]This is the title of the book of Duchrow (1993). Cf. also Duchrow (1994) and Duchrow (1995).

[38]Duchrow (1995), p. 29, pp. 42–47. Cf. also the argument for a world economic movement of citizens in Duchrow and Gück, p. 9.

[39]Cf. Duchrow (1995), pp. 21–38.

Chapter 3

Tradition and Context

Contextual theology has not yet shaped a new notion of tradition even if it has stressed the historical experience.

Urgent problems have led to base groups and theologians first reflecting upon the contemporary situation. Biblical interpretation has got an important function in understanding the situation. Tradition has been overlooked and the critics of liberation theology, therefore, have been able to voice disagreement from an alleged traditional interpretation of Christianity.

The interpretation of history should not end up in opposition to the interpretation of our contemporary times or of the future. Contextual theology ought to reflect upon the traditions of Christianity and the conditions of its interpretation to be able to develop claims for a comprehensive interpretation of Christianity.

The question is how contextual theology can shape a notion of tradition, which could stand close to experience and transcendence, i.e. the widening of the perspective.

As a first step, I reject an essentialist understanding of tradition, which is founded on the notion of that which has been remains current because it remains the same. Instead I advocate a dynamic view which is based on the notion of that which has been may remain current through its ability to "transcontextualize" itself. As a second step, I examine Robert J. Schreiter's model of a synthesis between tradition and local theology. Concluding, I will suggest three principles for the shaping of a trans-modern notion of tradition.

What "is" Tradition?

To put it simply, "traditions are the material of which culture have been made".[1] There is a difference between culture and tradition. The forms of tradition are on the one hand supra-cultural and on the other hand they are always dependent upon a cultural context. Tradition is what we hand over from one generation to another. This is something, which procreates in time and also in space. Traditions may also be handed over between different social classes.

If we shape the notion of tradition within a linear view of time, then the contents of tradition are joined to a special point on the string of time. History is then perceived as a series of events, which follow one upon the other. Tradition is what is handed over from one point on the line to another. Tradition is decided to be that which remains the same through different contexts of time.

Modernity has from the 19th century dynamically embodied this view of time. It is no longer the quality of a creature but its function in the process of time which will be the foremost characteristic of its life. You are what you achieve in time, and you realize yourself by what you achieve in history. Our modern notion of history arises at this time.

In modern times not only the subject is historically functionalized. The events, memories and objects from the past are instrumentalized too. Tradition becomes something, which must have a function. Thus arises the point of view that one may or may not have a tradition.

Modernity is characterized not only through decontextualization but it also brings a detraditionalization. People in the living world lose their immediate bonds to a given nature and cultural environment. They also lose the ties to the cultural expressions of past generations. The importance of both context and tradition, therefore, has to be continually created anew in the modern world.

The mobility on the labour market, for example, has the effect that no one can be sure of staying in the same place for a whole life. The exchange of information on the global media arena makes no tradition from the past or from another area obviously normative for one's own culture. That which is often called lack of tradition or history is rather an interlacing of particular traditions with modern urban ways of life. In common with the goods of the market, the particular traditions are tools in a supra-regional system of trade. Traditions are localized, transformed and exchanged in a looser anchoring in their earlier space and time.

Considering the modern situation, where tradition is what you make it, it seems unreasonable to continue claiming an essentialistic theological notion of tradition. Such a view of the Christian tradition means that one assumes that

- there is one tradition,

- what is handed over remains the same at different times and in different spaces,

- one is able to get unambiguous knowledge of the tradition as a whole, and

- this knowledge of tradition is normative for today's Christian interpretation of life.

Several objections ought to be raised against such a point of view. First, the thought of the unity of tradition is a social construction of those who interpret history of the past. A course of events is multifacetted and is difficult to access for that reason in its entirety.

Considering that events in the past only leave fragmentary traces, each researcher in history ought to constantly differ between history and the interpretation of history as well as between tradition and image of tradition. "History is thus an ongoing negotiation between the historian and the sources for what counts as history."[2]

Second, the notion of the single tradition's unity brings with it that which damages the integrity of history. The events of the past in this way become the objects of projecting particular interpretations of today. In colonial history, events involving women, nature systems and savages often happen in relation to tradition as well. The user reduces to objects, colonizes, reduces, instrumentalizes, and exploits the cultural inheritance according to his or her aims.

The history of theology also gives us proof of the Eurocentric exploitation of the traditions of the cultural inheritance. It is of less importance if the interpretations of Christian traditions are about Paul, Thomas or Luther. Common to a great part of historic theology of the 19th century, is the illusion of a possibility to gain unambiguous knowledge of how it "really" was or was thought to be. Then it was possible to conclude how it ought to be understood and how it ought to be tomorrow.

This essentialistic view of history one could denominate as being instrumentalized atomism. The atomist reduces the material of which cultures are made up to particles of dust, atoms, which supposedly are strung together on an imaginary string in time. The traditional theologian offers his reconstruction of something, which has been. Tradition becomes a tool of the theological construction of a normative interpretation of reality. The pastisches "liberal Jesus", "scholastic Thomas", or "Bible Luther" are offered as hermeneutical keys to the understanding of ongoing salvation history. Traditions become merchandise on a utilitarian market of ideas.

My criticism does not aim at cancelling the connection between the interpretation of traditions and normativity. A Christian interpretation of life without doubt ought to integrate the interpretation of past generation's theology, and it also ought to strive for an integration of Christian traditions of different geographic contexts. As a preface, I would just like to reject two current models of this interpretation of traditions. One seemingly allows tradition in its entirety to be within reach to reason, and the other instrumentalizes and reduces tradition out of hidden interests to use it.

Formulating it positively: theology firstly ought to supply arguments about why an event in the past is of importance to the future. Secondly, it ought to define which traditions are being interpreted and which importance is being attached to these, without normative arguments being construed with reference to "the" Christian tradition. Thirdly it ought to describe the intentions which affect its choice of objects and interpretations of tradition.

With such a point of view, there "is" no tradition, it only appears when someone conveys something to somebody. The act of handing over then leaves physical, social, and mental signs and traces in time and space. The agents of culture may interpret them or refrain from doing so. The signs in themselves can never become normative. Their interpretation, on the other hand, may become and ought to become important. The only question is how.

Tracy's Model of a "Correlation" between Tradition and Situation

David Tracy in association with Paul Tillich suggested that one could make use of a correlation hermeneutical model to interpret tradition. In short, this means that the theologian creates a "mutually critical correlation between tradition and situation". While Tillich departed from the point of view that the Christian tradition offers answers to the questions that the existential situation caused, Tracy develops a model which puts stress on the interaction of the two:

> *Theology is the attempt to establish mutually critical correlations*
> *between an interpretation of the Christian tradition and an inter-*
> *pretation of the contemporary situation.*[3]

My criticism of Tracy's thesis rests on him drawing a parallel to
the notions tradition and situation. When Tracy advocates a correlation between tradition on the one hand and situation on the other, he
seems to presume that tradition is something unambiguous and possibly something that remains unchanged. Even though Tracy is aware of
this being a hermeneutical challenge, I am not sure of the importance
to which he gives the criticism of tradition.

Rather, we ought to talk about a correlation between interpretations
of two different situations, for example between the Gospel according to
John and the Russian orthodox parishes of today, and then talk about
the correlation of interpretations of Christ-events in one or the other
context? Perhaps Tracy's notion of tradition threatens to bypass the
fact that languages, cultures and traditions change. Tracy's model perhaps accentuates continuity and identity at the expense of discontinuity
and inculturation.

Furthermore, Tracy argues that specific original sources in the history of theology should be seen as so-called "classics". My point of view
is that Tracy's classification projects strengthen my suspicion that he
represents a view of tradition which, according to some texts, are better
than others in expressing the content of tradition which always remains
the same.

A Dynamic Understanding of Tradition

Against Tracy's view of tradition, I will put forward a dynamic notion
of tradition, which differs from this in four ways:

- Tradition is not unified a priori, but it is composed of the different
  processes of handing-over in time. The whole of tradition is the
  sum of traces that these processes leave. The whole of the traditions to be sure is more than the sum. Tradition in its entirety
  remains unreachable to an ultimate understanding, though, as it
  is after all a question of an ongoing open process.

- Tradition does not distinguish itself through that which remains
  eternally the same, for instance the message of God's love for
  Creation. Instead it distinguish itself through both continuity
  and change. The continuity of tradition can only be upheld if

traditions are allowed to change in different processes of contextualization. What remains the same in tradition despite changes in conditions is that which has the ability to trans-contextualize itself. The criterion for time constant is, therefore, both a likeness in quality and acclimatization as well as an ongoing ability to in-culturate.

– It is only possible to get restricted but not unambiguous knowledge about tradition. The context of contemporary times and its conditions are the only prerequisites for the interpretation of history according to the sociology of knowledge. One should not strive for an interpretation of history, which is as objective as possible but one, which has the most context possible. The only means at hand are subjective and socially particular ways of getting close to historical sources.

– The notions of the normativity of theology ought not to be based on the assertion of the content of Christian tradition. Rather, they ought to be shaped in connection with the different traditions' approaches to problems, which are common to the past and present situation. If one is to carry through a normative correlation between a historical and a current situation, one ought to first identify the problem to be solved in both situations. Then one can correlate a situation's problem solving to the current situation. The older solution does not, a priori, have precedence over the younger. The normative keys are generated not by the interpretation of tradition but by the interaction game between the interpretation of tradition and situation.[4] Tradition only wins a normative character when it has proven capable of being conveyed.

The Sociocultural Memory of Local Theologies

The North American theologian Robert J. Schreiter has developed an approach to Christian tradition which does not presuppose that the contents of handing over remain the same. His outlook on tradition is well suited to contextual theology.

Schreiter characterizes the church's tradition as a "series of local theologies".[5] He differentiates historically between four theological ways of expression and they are: variations of a holy text, wisdom, knowledge and praxis.[6] These expressions arise within particular cultural contexts.

As an example, theology as science arose in a social transition period where the agricultural economy was urbanized in competition with the Arabic trade and production system and where universities developed to provide for society's demands for a differentiated working life education. Relations between tradition and culture are dialectic interactions to Schreiter in which the local theology comes into being.[7] The themes of theology develop out of the interpretation of the cultural situation and its document. Tradition is interpreted and the picture of a series of local theologies develops.

Each local Christian theology is connected with Christian tradition. On the one hand, this tradition has an influence on the development of the local theology. On the other hand, each local theology has an effect on tradition as it both forgets and remembers and, in this way, contributes to handing over in the future. The local theology also influences its own cultural situation. Culture and tradition depend upon each other and simultaneously change each other interactively.

Schreiter assumes that tradition still promotes the human feeling of solidarity. It offers possibilities of identity, it creates a coherent and time constant system of communication and it makes the incorporation of renewal possible.[8]

Schreiter develops his theory linguistically. He applies Noam Chomsky's distinction between "competence" and "performance" and applies Chomsky's generative grammar to the Christian tradition.[9]

Tradition, therefore, signifies "the entire language system". "Faith" and "theology" are the equivalent of "language competence" and the "loci of orthodoxy" is the equivalent of the grammar, which mediates between competence and performance.[10] Tradition is to Schreiter a language system. Its grammar is dynamic.

Against Schreiter it may be said that it is hardly possible to draw a parallel between the linguistic competence of culture and faith. Firstly, the competence of faith includes not only linguistic expressions but also images and other aesthetic ways of expression.[11] The handing over of these follow other patterns than those of the language. Secondly, there is a conflict in the context of secularization between the cultural language competence and the language of faith. One could possibly compare the competence of religious language to other forms of language.

It is further unclear how Schreiter means that a theological proposition interacts with the development of grammar. As an example, we may cite the Nicean Constantinopolitan Council's decision regarding the importance of the Holy Spirit in the year 381. It is clear that the theology of Gregory of Nazianz influenced the Council. But what do we know about the influence of the Council on later views of the Spirit in other theological contexts?

In spite of this criticism, the following three arguments support Schreiter's view on tradition:

- It excludes a static point of view, as it does not operate with the distinction between "the tradition" and "traditions". Tradition is viewed as a result of events in handing over. This result is not only the sum of the contents of handing over, but it constitutes the language system of the Christian faith. I would prefer to call this language system "the sociocultural memory" of the faithful.[12] This memory originates both in the social interaction and in the cultural, coded handing over of events.

- According to Schreiter's view, we cannot look on tradition as a criterion of truth for Christian assertions of faith.[13] Each theology arises within a culturally conditioned situation, and each tradition is a result of the handing over of local theologies.[14] With this point of view, it is not possible to elevate the interpretation of one local theology as a norm over the other. The conception of what constitutes the entirety of tradition remains open. That which characterizes the collective series of local theologies remains a constant challenge in interpretation to each local theology. The local theology must create catholicity in dialogue with the past generation's theology for the sake of coming generations.

- A third reason to adopt the dynamic and contextual notion of tradition lies in the importance of the future for the concept of tradition. Each local theology affects the development of its cultural context as well. Thereby it is set in an irreversible time process. Each interpretation of tradition ultimately aims at the shaping of the formation of the future fellowship. To preserve the flow in the handing over process, we ought to observe the importance of the future for the interpretation of tradition. Memory of the past always fills the function of being able to meet that which is coming. Living creatures seldom remember for the sake of history but mostly for the sake of their own survival. In this sense, the sociocultural memory has a function, which is decided by the conditions in point.

It is important to reflect upon the interests of power, which have an influence on the interpretation of tradition since the context is conditioned by the descriptions of tradition. Since tradition creates future possibilities of life, it is suitable to a high degree for strengthening and expanding power positions. If church history from the perspective of the winner is not to be confused with the Christian tradition itself, that is, with the sociocultural memory in the perspective of the liberated people, then one needs to include an analysis of power in the interpretation of Christianity's social and cultural memory.

According to my view, tradition is not just a series of local theologies as Schreiter claims but a sociocultural memory that helps the fellowships of believers to preserve series of local theologies.[15]

Three Principles in a Contextual Interpretation of Tradition

What is the aim of the criticism of tradition in contextual theology? How can we shape interpretations of the social and cultural memory where the faithful remember series of local theologies, which do not reduce and instrumentalize tradition?

By way of conclusion, I will suggest three principles for the interpretation of contextual tradition. They can be summed up in three theses:

- Traditions in the cultural environment of human beings and the natural environment are parts of one single common biospherical history.

- When interpreting this history we ought to give precedence to those living on the underside of culture and history of nature.

- When interpreting history for the sake of the future, we ought to correct the modern description of progress and growth and their tradition. This could be done through a trans-modern statement of the traditions of the victims and losers. The durability of tradition's interpretation will appear in its practical relevance.

Traditions as Part of One Sole Biospherical History

In the Latin American theology of liberation, Gustavo Gutiérrez has emphasized the principle of one sole common history. In this history both the oppressor and the victim are participants. Because of this, also the experiences of the victims will be heard. A just perspective of historical events comes into being only when experiences on the underside of history become part of the interpretation of history.

According to my belief, this principle ought to be expanded from social history to history of nature. Human society is still thoroughly dependent on nature and the process of evolution continuing. The culture of humankind is embedded in the nature of the planet. Here, we can understand culture as a special contribution to the biosphere's life. Human social history, therefore, makes a part of natural history.

In the ecological challenge this connection appears especially painful. The world community has plunged into a global ecological crisis, as it no longer knows how its modernization affects future biological life processes. The history of nature is nowadays totally included in the history of modern economic world system. The victims that this system harvests exist both in society and in the ecosystem of nature. We can, therefore, talk about "the poor" existing both in culture and in nature. As I see it, a liberation theology that strives to hold forward the social victims' perspectives on their historical experiences also should strive to give voice to the suppressed organisms in the ecosystem. Theology in the late modern ecological challenge ought to be designed as ecological liberation theology.

Ecological criticism of Christianity asserts that the Jewish Christian interpretation of Creation legitimizes an unjust exploitation of natural resources. We should object to this and point out that modern exploitation of natural resources has accelerated thanks to the social utopia of the enlightenment and the applied technical sciences of nature. Christianity's theologically reduced view of the world had, at this time, already lost its normative influence on the relations to nature. It seems rather reasonable to accuse Christian theology of not having contributed sufficiently to the shaping of a global ethic of the environment. This would have shielded the victims during the fateful modernization of relations to nature.

Considering our question about the importance of the notion of tradition, the task will be describing the history of the growth of modern society in the light of exploitation of the victims of nature. What organisms in culture and nature's ecosystem have fallen victim to the power of evil? How does the belief that God creates, supports and liberates everything between heaven and earth relate to this history? What traditions of the created beings' hope and waiting for liberation lie hidden in the sociocultural memory of Christianity?

The principle of one sole common biospherical history, which encompasses both suppressors and victims in cultural and natural history, leads to the demand that the suppressed and invisible experiences are part of the interpretation of traditions.

The Tradition of the Silenced

The second principle asserts priority to those on the underside of history when interpreting tradition.

In his text "Über den Begriff der Geschichte", Walter Benjamin carries on a controversy against the historian who wishes to know "how it really was".[16] Benjamin places the true picture of the past which "whizzes by" against the interpretation of history of the current powers.[17] Not even the history of the dead is safe to the victorious enemy's interpretation of history. According to Benjamin, the materialist "will rub history the right way".

Benjamin places "the tradition of the suppressed" as a condition for a new notion of history.[18] This is in contrast to the notion of history's advancements. Historically, one ought not to depict "the eternal picture of the past" but "an experience of the past".[19]

Benjamin's text challenges theology and the Christian view of tradition. His thesis that the oppressed has other knowledge of tradition than the victor has, refers Christianity to the centre of its sociocultural memory and to the memory of the Messiah who suffered and failed. We can learn from Benjamin about the conditions of the knowledge of the oppressed tradition:

> It is not given to each and everyone, in each place and at each time but only at the moment of danger.[20]

Knowledge about the difference between the interpretations of history, that also could be developed sociologically leads to the tradition of the oppressed being a leading theme to theological hermeneutics This hermeneutics builds on the memory of Christ's suffering. Pneumatologically, the Holy Spirit is regarded as the one who gave possibility to this memory.

The memory of the history of God's suffering, of the history of martyrs in the Early Church and of the victims in the history of the church and in present times becomes, according to this point of view, a necessary condition for the knowledge of salvation history.[21]

If in this way we develop the notion of tradition in the light of the Trinity and the Cross, then we allot the suppressed theoretical preference for knowledge at the actualization of the Christian tradition. As the tradition of the suppressed is not exactly accessible to everyone, the question arises which subjects that could gain knowledge of this tradition. The tradition of the suppressed exists "for those at present poor and despairing and only in the places where they suffer, only in their vicinity".[22] They have great cause to believe and to hope for, to experience and reflect upon the liberating acts of God because of their exposed situation.

I would also award the suffering beings on the underside of history a function at the interpretation of tradition like the poor people in the history of society. The ecological victims of cultural violence ought to be included in the tradition of the suppressed as well.

With such an outlook the liturgical formation of religious communities would also be able to make biological species visible and their agony in the fight for survival. They would be able to interpret the memory of species that perished in the cultural colonial history in the light of St Paul's speech about the created beings partaking in human suffering and liberation.[23] These species have, in common with the martyrs, suffered for the sake of their Saviour. The memory of their fight for survival gets an important function in the ecological theology of liberation. The hope of rising from the dead also applies to them.

The Criticism of the Tradition of Progress and the Practical Relevance of Tradition

The third principle for a contextual interpretation of tradition implies the demand for the criticism of modern tradition of progress.

According to Max Horkheimer and Theodor W. Adorno, modernity is distinguished by a dialectic where some people are made victims. Modernity is founded in 1492 when, according to Enrique Dussel, the encapsulated Europeans placed Europe in the middle of the world map thanks to Spain. They turned the Amerindian peoples into victims of world trade and the progress of world mission.[24] A couple of years later, "America" is invented which serves as a construction of Europe's "other".

Dussel shows this history partly out of the perspective of the discoverers and partly of that of the victims, the Amerindians. What appears to be liberation and progress for one culture signifies sacrifice and ruin for another.

The Cherokee theologian George Tinker talks about "cultural genocide" and holds the mission co-responsible.[25] The natives themselves see this much clearer than the conquerors. They grasp the invasion primarily as the return of the gods and then they interpret the fall as an apocalypse at the end of "the era of the fifth sun".[26]

According to Dussel, Europe never was capable of discovering the real face of the other. It saw instead only a mirror object in the opposite culture. "The other is the same."[27] From his historical analysis of the anti-liberating history of mission, Dussel concludes that tomorrow' s task is at the same time to complete the emancipatory development and eliminate its myth of violence, which asserts that its progress demands that some people are violently sacrificed.

Dussel's way of thinking should be extended to all of the victims of modernization: African, Asian, Polynesian, Australian tribes and people's cultures, women in all of the cultures, ecosystems in areas prone to ruthless colonial exploitation. The myth of sacrifice of the modern project's progress has many faces: androcentrism makes women victims, Christian Eurocentrism erases all other cultures and religions, and modern antropocentrism sacrifices nature. The connection between the different types of violence was summed up already in 1940 by the Swedish author Elin Wägner: Peace on earth and reconciliation between the sexes implies peace with earth.[28]

As a principle, the criticism of the myth of progress from an inter-pretation of traditions of the others also leads to a practical readiness. Christianity may be characterized as a religion with high ability for transformation and inculturation. Its history stays alive because its tradition trans-contextualizes itself.

If religion today would like to meet the other in religious pluralism, then it can learn from experience about its own history of inculturation in the Hellenistic culture. The synthesis of Christian and Greek, which often is painted black, has not yet impaired the core of the Gospel. This was earlier claimed for confessional reasons. On the contrary, Chris-tianity created critical syntheses with stoicism (Tertullian, Irenaeus), gnosticism (Origenes), and neo-platonism (Augustine and the Cappado-cians), the conditions for the spread of Christianity after Constantine.

These syntheses were not firstly based upon the theoretical evidence of the interpretation of faith. We should rather interpret the incultur-ation of Christianity and the transformation of the culture of antiquity as a mutual acknowledgement of the Christian image of God and of the world and also the emancipating social praxis of the church, where victims, slaves and strangers occupied a prominent place. The ancient church's theology expresses the experience of following the Jewish peo-ple's inheritance of being a "contrast society".[29] This tradition is best expressed in the love for the poor.[30]

To my mind, the historical insight leads contextual interpretation to a necessary demand for practical relevance of the Christian faith for the other. According to this point of view, tradition is the sociocultural memory, which influences the interaction between idea and behaviour.

Handing-over is only a fact when the Christian tradition is brought to the fore and becomes relevant for the transformation of the life-worlds of people.

Summary

- Contextual theology has clearly accented the historical experience, but it has not yet shaped a new notion of tradition. Tradition has been put in the shadow and the critics of liberation theology therefore have been able to raise objections from an alleged traditional interpretation of Christianity. If contextual theology should lay claims to an extensive interpretation of Christianity and to a liberating relevance, then it ought to develop a reflection of the tradition of Christianity.

- An essential and modernistic view of history and tradition is not suitable for this project as it emanates from four characteristics:

  - that tradition is one,
  - that which is handed over remains the same in different times and places,
  - that we can get unambiguous knowledge of tradition as a whole, and
  - that this knowledge of tradition in itself is normative for Christian interpretation today.

The essentialistic view is rejected in favour of a dynamic and trans-modern view in which:

  - Tradition is not a priori homogeneous but is composed of various processes of handing-over in time,
  - tradition is not distinguished by what remains perpetually the same but by its ability to trans-contextualize itself through changing states in time,
  - we cannot obtain unambiguous knowledge of tradition but only restricted such,
  - the notion of tradition does not by itself lay the foundation of normative assertions about the current Christian interpretation of life.

- The American theologian Robert J. Schreiter's approach to tradition is well suited to contextual theology. He categorizes the church's tradition as a "series of local theologies". In spite of a certain criticism, there are three reasons for following Schreiter:

  - His view of tradition does not operate with the distinction between "the tradition" and "traditions". Tradition is instead viewed as a consequence of courses of events in handing things over. This course of events is not only the sum of the content of handing-over but is, according to Schreiter, the language system of the Christian faith. I would rather call this language system the "sociocultural memory" of the faithful.

  - According to Schreiter's outlook, one cannot regard tradition as a truth-criteria of Christian postulates. What characterizes the collected series of local theologies remains a constant interpretation challenge for each local theology. The local theology must create catholicity in a dialogue with the theology of the past generations for the sake of coming generations.

  - A third reason lies in the importance of the future for the notion of tradition. Each interpretation aims ultimately at shaping the form of the future fellowship.

The Christian tradition is thereby not only a series of local theologies (Schreiter) but a social and cultural memory which helps the fellowships of the holy to actualize series of local theologies for the sake of their future.

- Three principles ought to lead the way in the contextual interpretation of tradition:

  - Traditions in the cultural environment of humanity and the life environment of nature ought to be seen as parts of one, sole, common biospherical history.

  - At the interpretation of this history precedence should be given to those living on the underside of cultural and natural history, i.e. the "silenced traditions".

  - At the interpretation of history for the future, the tradition of development and growth ought to be corrected through a trans-modern representation of the traditions of victims and losers. The tenability of the interpretation of tradition shows up in its practical relevance for survival.

Notes

[1] Honko, p. 16.

[2] Merchant, p. 4

[3] Tracy (1986), p. 234. Cf. Tracy (1985), p. 36.

[4] Cf. Bergmann (1995a), Chapter VI.1.

[5] Schreiter p. 32, p. 93. For an extensive discussion of Schreiters approach see Bevans, pp. 85–88, and Bergmann (1995a), Chapter VI.2.

[6] Schreiter, pp. 80–93.

[7] Schreiter, p. 25.

[8] Schreiter, p. 105.

[9] Cf. Chomsky, p. 14–15.

[10] Schreiter, p. 115.

[11] Cf. Irvin who gives all his attention to the significance of interpretation of the scripture for the relationship of catholicity and contextuality. Hereby he remains in the protestant text-orientated culture which overlooks other aesthetical forms of communicating traditions. A wider contextual study of history should to a greater extent attend non-literary processes of handing over traditions.

[12] On the notions of "social memory" and "cultural memory" see Cavalli, pp. 207–208. Cf. also the notion "collective memory" of Halbwachs who develops the thesis that the images of the past become objects of conflict between different social groups. The interpretation of the notion of tradition with the help of the notion of memory can already be observed in the 16th century. See Wiedenhofer, pp. 626–627.

[13] Against Kasper, p. 399, who regards traditions as an actualization of the one tradition and who offers a typological-sacramental understanding of tradition.

[14] Schreiter, p. 115.

[15] Bergmann (1995a), pp. 366–369.

[16]Benjamin, p. 695.

[17]Benjamin, p. 695.

[18]Benjamin, p. 69.

[19]Benjamin, p. 702.

[20]John (1991), p. 76.

[21]Cf. Metz' important and strongly discussed essay on the significance of the rememberance of Christ's suffering for the theological understanding of society.

[22]John (1988), p. 524.

[23]"... because the creature itself also shall be delivered from the bondage of corruption into the glory's liberty of the children of God." (Romans 8,20–21) St Paul relates here to a tradition where also the non-human nature takes part in God's history of salvation. Cf. the evangelist's telling about the sun's, the darkness' and the earth's participation in Christ's death on the cross on Golgatha: Mark 15,33 (Cf. Amos 8,9), Matthew 27,45-53, Luke 23,44f.

[24]Dussel, pp. 15–16.

[25]Tinker, pp. 5–8.

[26]Dussel, pp. 121–122, p. 161.

[27]Dussel, p. 42.

[28]Wägner and Tamm.

[29]N. Lohfink, p. 118, G. Lohfink, pp. 55–57. Cf. Duchrow (1994), pp. 134–140.

[30]Gregory of Nazianz, Oratio 14.5.

Chapter 4

Knowledge and Context

The approach to knowledge has changed in our late modern age. The theories of knowledge that since the age of enlightenment have been representing universal claims to the truth are under reappraisal. It no longer seems evident why a universal theory of the essence of knowledge is possible, meaningful, and on the whole desirable.

Historically I interpret the transformation of the approach to knowledge as a stage in the ongoing process of social modernization, which at the present time includes the entire globe with its culture and nature. In a further historical perspective, this transformation is embedded in a process of colonization going back at least five hundred years with its startingpoint in Central European geography and way of thinking.

In spite of all proclamations of its end, a sociological analysis shows that the modernization of the social structures, the relations to nature and the ways of thinking continue. The late modernization constitutes a global course of events, which incorporates the planet's cultures and ecosystems under the hegemony of a single economic world system. The omnipotence of this world system is founded on the handling of money and ideology. There are many in society and in nature who become victims of this world power.

It seems to me rather a hopeful sign that intellectuals in this situation critically reconsider the current approach to knowledge and its effects. The manifold in the approach to knowledge in this way contributes to correcting the "foolishness" in the economic world system's extensive claims to power. Criticism of objective truth and knowledge theories do not necessarily lead to a relativistic and elitist view of knowledge.[1] It may also lead to a third position, to contextualism.[2]

The aim of this chapter is to give a picture of the ongoing conversion of the approach to knowledge as a challenge to pastoral and academic theology. Some reasons will be given why the contextual approach to knowledge creates a new paradigm for theology. The train of thought is shaped with special regard to Per Frostin's contribution to the discussion of theology's approach to knowledge.

The New View of Knowledge

We can discern four characteristics in the emerging approach to knowledge.

The Subject of Knowledge

The question of the subject of knowledge and its social context comes to the foreground.

While older epistemology departed from a static and monist outlook on humankind, current attempts call our attention to the interaction between the subject and his/her social and ecological context, which affect the production of knowledge. The focus is partly on the specific in the constellation of subject and context and partly on the differences to other constellations. Since the age of Nietzsche, ever-increasing importance is attached to the perspective character of knowledge. The experiences of and the insights into the specific, the contrasting and the perspective shape new ways of achieving and producing knowledge.

Feminist gender studies emphasize the specific in women's way of shaping and expressing knowledge of humankind and society.[3] Theology in the South brings out the importance of "the third world experience". The theology of liberation emphasizes the poor and the suppressed as important partners in discussions as they own a specific capability of perceiving and interpreting conflicts and solutions. In the ecological movement, people make themselves representatives for the organisms and surrounding worlds threatened by cultural violence. Human ecological anthropology shows the importance of the ecological context for the individual and social creation of opinion.

The Social Context of Knowledge

The important question for the philosophy of enlightenment was that of the essence of knowledge. This has now been displaced to a question of social context and function of knowledge. The new view on knowledge does not presuppose an outlook on humankind that assumes a kind of human substance in which reason remains the same at all times and in all places. It assumes rather that the subject of knowledge constitutes itself through a large number of social factors in its cultural context, like gender, wealth, class, tradition, potential for development etc. The anthropological essentialism is discarded in favour of a relational view on the human person. His/her body and thinking are constituted through interaction with both his/her biological and sociocultural environment.

The view on humankind and knowledge is now being integrated in the view on society. Knowledge is determined rather as a communicative function, for example as an interplay between competence and performance, than as a result of an inherent human characteristic.

The sociology of knowledge paraphrases this function with the notion "social construction of reality",[4] and it analyses how circumstances in society affect the subject's handling of information, knowing and knowledge. Communication philosophy joins together the previously incompatible empirical and transcendental positions. It replaces the question of the nature of knowledge with the question of knowledge's social connection and of rationality in communicative social course of events.

The Method of Making Knowledge

A third feature is found in the view of method. The insight of Paul Tillich, that "methodical imperialism is as dangerous as political imperialism"[5] is now fully assimilated. Neither empirical nor hermeneutic methods may be said to lead to insights that automatically give them a universal character. Neither empiricism nor hermeneutics are allowed to be ideologies. Deductive and inductive methods do not confront each other but are linked together in new method developments. Interpretations of historical material are qualitatively no different than contemporary material, so they can be linked together by, for example, the correlation method.

In our Nordic anthologies "Contextual Interpretation of Life" and "Theology of Everyday Culture"[6] it can be concluded how different methods that come into being in different theological traditions in the Nordic countries, may be applied within a common framework of discussion. The anthologies show how empirical, hermeneutic, analytic, sociological, phenomenological and correlative methods are applied to treating the reciprocal action between material, problem, context and practice.

Another important insight is offered by the history of art and aesthetics, which draws the attention of the text-oriented and behaviour-oriented social sciences to the importance of intuition and image thinking.

The art historian, Sven Sandström, shows in his theory how image thinking proceeds as "significance creating" in a "space of meaning".[7] Image thinking does not stand equal side by side with linear discursive thinking. Instead it differs structurally and qualitatively from the latter. As "lucidity", image thinking appears as a spatial constellation while "discursively" it is in progress as a digital confrontation. Sandström shows how the image experience related to the creation of sense and the intuitive memory matter constitutes the prerequisite of verbal linguistics, as this itself does not "contain" anything but only acts in relation to meanings.

Thinking in images and intuitively treating and understanding does not constitute an alternative to the logical discourse. Linguistic thinking ought rather to be understood as a completion of image thinking which aims at correlation with the earlier notion of learning. According to Sandström, a theory of significations and the creation of signification may not presuppose the verbal language to begin with but has to develop independently of the linguistic approach to reality.

According to this insight, a new approach to learning may not naturally presuppose the language but ought to assume that the creation of signification and meaning takes place within a complex process of experiences and inner image creation. The linguistic interpretation process would not be possible without the production of the inner visual pictures for orientation. It should become evident that the physical surrounding world of the subject as well as his/her memory world gets an important and often overseen function.

Problem-oriented Knowledge

A fourth feature refers to choice of problem for scientific study. In a contextual approach to knowledge, the scientific elite deprives itself of the priority to choose problems. The process of problem-formulation becomes public to an increased extent. A problem for academic study ought to be, in the first place, a problem for others. It may be said by using a quote by the Asian theologian Kosuke Koyama, (at a lecture in Malmö, Sweden, January 1994): "Too many academic theologians answer questions that no one has put." The research process is preceded by a socially plausible argumentation in which and for whom the problem exists and what its solution could mean for those concerned.

The science philosopher Nicholas Maxwell argues for the necessity of a "new, more rigorous kind of inquiry" which lends priority to those problems and solutions that are important for everybody's life.[8] Maxwell differs between problem-solving and aim-pursuing rationality. He proposes basic rules and connects the methodology of the social and natural sciences. The new research that Maxwell strives for consists of both a "philosophy of knowledge" which includes the two above-mentioned rationalities and a "philosophy of wisdom". While the philosophy of knowledge should help create a better world, the task of the philosophy of wisdom consists of implementing the rules of the philosophy of knowledge. Wisdom is to Maxwell "the capacity to realize what is of value in life".[9] Maxwell mentions work with the question "How can we best learn how to realize what is of value?"[10] as a basic problem for his wisdom philosophy of knowledge.

This attempt is interesting for two reasons in this connection. It is partly because it clearly emphasizes the significance of the argument process around the question why an academic problem is a problem. The questions it poses are: Who are those who are involved in the problem and how does the process of knowledge constitute a solution to the problem? It is partly because the scientist is well aware of the need to complete current research rationality with something we may loosely call wisdom, metaphysics, values, worldview and religion. How can theology contribute to the discussion about the need for new wisdom in science?

The Challenge to a Theological Approach to Knowledge

Four Questions

In connection to the four characteristics above, theology is challenged by treating four questions:

- Which discussion partner do the agents in academic systematic theology choose and why?

  Men or women, rich or poor, well-formulated or suppressed, classics or colleagues, church, academy or society, institutions, wealthy people or Non-Governmental Organisations?

  Liberation theology argues in favour of giving the poor priority within the theoretical discourse. Feminist theology is in favour of giving women preference when in situations of injustice caused by gender. Ecological theology argues for giving priority to oppressed

nature.[11] I summarize these three groups under the common de-
nominator "the suppressed" knowing well that a clarification of
criteria is still necessary.

By priority I do not mean that the suppressed themselves possess
greater insights into the truth and, therefore, earn their priority,
but rather that they have special qualities for insights into the
truth. The theological discourse parts with if it does not look after the perspective of the poor. "Priority" in the first place means
"admittance" to the theological discourse and in the second place
the right of speech while the till-then privileged only listen. The
aim with the thesis of preference to the poor consists of extending
the discourse so that more experiences will be heard and then, especially, the specifically qualified experiences. In such a discourse,
the severing of perspective does not lead to relativism and nihilism
but to a reciprocally enriched communicative contextualism.

The basic assumption is that the plurality in a common discourse
qualitatively increases the shape and content of discourse as well
as it increases its chances of universalizing its consensus.

– Which function belongs to the analysis of context in theological
  interpretation process?

Per Frostin mentions three such functions for the analysis of context:[12] i) it is used as a heuristic tool, that is, like an instrument
to detect hidden and hard to understand contexts and messages
in theological expressions; ii) it works as a critical principle and
prevents by analysis both a false centring on the interpreter as
well as a misguided idealization of the other; iii) it challenges the
interpreter to new self-understanding.

– How is the significance of methodical pluralism valued within Religious Studies and in the interdisciplinary scientific exchange of
  theories and methods? How is a development of methods aided,
  which satisfies the balance between logically discursively thinking
  and image thinking, and between intuition and understanding in
  image and analysis as well as interpretation in words?

– How does the academic organization practically meet the need of
  a new orientation around the essential problems in our age, and
  how does it develop criteria for an examination of the problem
  relevance when planning and applying theological research? The
  challenge concerns the relation to other agents in academia as well

as to other agents in society, in the popular movements, the institutions, the communions and the market. How does theology orient itself around formulated problems that give the suppressed priority? How do the suppressed win a constructive function within systematic theology?

Six Criteria in the Approach to Theology's Knowledge by Per Frostin

Departing from the texts by Per Frostin, I will use six theses in his theological contribution to shed light on contextual theology's new approach to knowledge.

The Political Hermeneutics

Each text from the past or from other contexts in the world is understood through interpretation. Each such understanding is set in a political context. The materialistic interpretation of the Bible and the reformation is superior to the idealistic. Hermeneutics (the theory of interpretation) is political and politics is hermeneutic.

In his dissertation, Frostin shows that there is a "structural bond" between hermeneutics and politics, between understanding a text and the social situation.[13] He studies Bultmann and Luther in the light of each other. Frostin is interested both in their interpretations of the Bible and in their interpretations of their contemporary political situation.

He uncovers contrasts between Luther and Bultmann which lead him to the question: If reality and history are one, how is it then possible to claim that God appears in two spaces? How can we claim that God is Saviour beyond the world when we only possess knowledge of this world?

One of the driving forces seems to be preserving the Bible text and Luther's theology as important sources and implements for the understanding and attaining of political liberation. At the time of upheaval before and after 1968, when the dissertation was written, the battle was on two fronts at the same time.

It was partly about settling accounts with the theologians, who upheld the authority of Luther through quoting without bothering to understand what they read. The other objective was to justify, in an increasingly secular society, that Christian faith on the whole could contribute to the political battle.

Frostin was successful on both fronts. The theologians of "repristina-tion"[14] today can no longer claim science in academia or fidelity to the creed in church. In contrast to the 1970s, the Christian contributions on the political arena are more in demand than ever.[15]

The political hermeneutics can be summed up as follows: Each in-terpretation of text and tradition is embedded in and decided by its political context. It is impossible to interpret as if one were "beyond the world".

The Context

> *Each piece of knowledge is determined by the context within which*
> *it originates. No person can attain general eternal knowledge.*
> *What we "know" depends upon how reality is constructed in so-*
> *ciety.*[16]

Each piece of knowledge is determined by its context. If each per-son is part of a social whole, then this naturally also affects his/her knowledge. This is not to say that the individual is only guided by social constructions, by values, trends and information. The individual also exerts an influence on what others know and on what makes others know or not know, respectively.

The theory of knowledge sociology implies that knowledge is always created in a social context, which can be a school, a parliament, a newspaper or a parish. Nobody knows something alone. That which constitutes our knowledge is experienced by others, shared by others and is communicated to others. The context is common and this causes knowledge to be divided. Therefore it ensues that no individual may claim access to the one, true item of knowledge.

Frostin applied this insight by comparing Christian belief in God to the belief in the market forces. The market constructs its view on reality, and its approach to knowledge and humanity. In the image of the reality of the market no God is necessary. Men and women are economic creatures, who buy, sell, exchange, consume and produce. "In this context religion also becomes an investment."[17] On the other hand, Christian faith expresses another view about human beings. They are part of Creation and not only of the market. Men and women create through the power of God and not through their own power. Faith in the market shields from the dark sides of life and suffering. Christian faith chooses instead the road to life through death.[18]

The Wholeness

Reality is one. History is one. The fact that knowledge is decided by particular contexts does not mean that reality is shattered. The challenge of pluralism signifies seeking the narrow road between relativism and uncritical universality.

Frostin wrote in several contexts in the late 1970s about "the African view of the whole". We may assume that his stay in Africa meant significant discoveries of the connections of life's entirety.

Today, entirety has become ideology and is called "holism" and sometimes also "monism".

What Frostin and many others were opposing was the splitting up of reality. According to this thinking, there should be one space for God, one for man/woman, one for believers, one for atheists, one for nature, and one for history. Scientists cut up history in periods that conditionally were threaded like pearls on a time-string. At pleasure history could begin with Jesus, St Augustine, Luther or Mao. This approach to history and nature is today successfully proclaimed dead.

The thesis that reality and history is one was aimed at those who claimed precedence for the interpretation of the contemporary age and, above all, history. The thesis of Frostin implied that the history of Christianity is a common gift. The historiography of theology was not allowed to place selectively and normatively certain parts over others like, for instance, pietism and confessional Lutheran orthodoxy over the Reformation and the Early Church. These events should instead be interpreted in the light of Christianity' s situation of today.

The Swedish theologian Gustaf Wingren, met the same opponents with his thesis about it being the exposition of Luther's message, which should throw light upon modern times. Frostin took a more difficult road. According to him, the interpretation of Luther and the current situation was what would shape the interpretation of Christianity and, finally, the image of God. To him it was as earlier to Gustaf Aulén, God was active in the "still today", not as Law but as Liberator. It can be said rather in a polemic way: with Wingren, God is active through the innate power of Creation and the preachings of the church. With Frostin, God is active through people's political answer to the Gospels in action.[19]

They both assumed that reality and history was one, namely that of the Creator and Saviour. They both were of the opinion that if history and reality were God's, then the demand for "catholicity", and not only in this meaning but above all universality, under any circumstances could not be abandoned.

The question remained: How can the Christian and the church endure both believing and knowing when simultaneously living in shattered and irreconcilable contexts? How should one "share God's attitude against the devil" (P.E. Persson)? How and to what life does God liberate?

The Divergency

> *Experiences in the social context influence knowledge. Experiences of conflict, especially, lead to discoveries. There is a marked difference between knowledge from above and from downwards. Those who have experiences from the dark- and underside of life, have another outlook on reality than rich, powerful and educated people.*

Frostin repeatedly accentuated that liberation theology has developed a new approach to knowledge. This thesis is a difficult challenge for the critics. If the thesis is correct, the question arises in which meaning knowledge was true. Is it the poor people's knowledge or that of the rich?

The critics of liberation theology mostly evade this problem and play down the thesis about poor people's knowledge. One position asserts that there is nothing catholic anyway. Each individual knows best and each and everyone uses his/her knowledge as well as possible. Success may show this to be true or false.

Another position asserts that in the third world one simply has misunderstood the claim of the West to have the only view on knowledge. The prerequisites for knowledge are always the same. They never change. They are possibly linguistically determined, but the contextual and the change are played down. Accordingly, the differences between the cultures are distorted. We are all humans, as the saying goes. Pluralism is not a problem. The rich nations assert the prerogative of deciding what is true and false.

A third position accepts the thesis of the new understanding of life but does not dare take the consequences for their own life. The attitude is rather to let the knowledge of the poor stay with the poor. Liberation theology is a matter for the third world and not the first. It may be that the Somali woman's knowledge is of another kind than that of the Swedish theologian. Her knowledge does not constitute a challenge to me, does it?

The first position denies the thesis of the challenge of the poor people's knowledge. The second position denies or relativizes the thesis. The third agrees theoretically but in practice applies the second position. A fourth position accepts the challenge and in meetings with the poor tries their knowledge.

Identification

The experience of the suppressed in the world around us is equivalent to the suppressed experiences within us. Liturgy and diaconia constitute a practice where the knowledge of our suppressed neighbour, and that which is suppressed within us, is transformed into liberation.

In his essay on God or mammon, Frostin wrote:

To attach one's heart to God is to discover people who are suppressed but also discover the suppressed parts of oneself.

Luther's definition of a God was "the one you attach your heart to". The Christian belief in God as the one you attach your heart to, signifies discovering the suppressed fellow creatures and, in that way, discover the suppressed part of oneself.

For Frostin this was a late discovery. I remember that in his teaching he talked about the inner shadows in man and woman, and that justification through faith in modern language could be interpreted as humans being seen by God, even with their dark sides.

I call this the identification criterion. The suffering one sees and understands in one's surroundings corresponds with what is blacked-out, repressed and invisible within one. Such a discovery later makes possible practical identification and solidarity between rich and poor.

A simple example is given: Imagine that you encounter a policeman who is maltreating a demonstrator in South Africa. You may then choose to close your eyes, escape or step in. If you have been beaten yourself maybe as a child your memory may help you choose. You may remember that you coped with it then and you step in. You may repress the memory and then you flee. But if you actively side with the person maltreated, he or she may also help you to get to know something new. You see the memory of your own maltreatment in a new light. If you can solve the conflict with the policeman together you may be freed from your own anxiety. The victim is saved and perhaps even the policeman learns something new.

In another context, this thought is behind Frostin's and my anthology "God of the silenced". Knowledge of the poor in the third world teaches us something new about the poor here at home and ultimately about what is blacked-out within us. Christian diaconia, in the sense of human synergy with God for liberation, occurs for the sake of life.

In a third context, Frostin deepens this dimension in knowledge within the field of mysticism, contemplation and prayer. Unfortunately he was not allowed to continue the path towards a liberating spirituality where he could have intertwined the three threads of knowledge, struggle and prayer to a stronger rope.

Now where was the Christian message in the different contributions of Frostin to the new approach to knowledge? An answer is hinted at in the sixth criteria "The love for the poor".

The Love for the Poor

The love for the poor is an expression of love for God. This love
leads to giving preference to the knowledge of the poor.

How can love be a contribution to knowledge? Is not he who loves blind? Frostin himself chose not to express it so: "the love for the poor". This is my way to summarize his approach with the term $(\Phi\iota\lambda o\pi\tau\omega\chi\iota\alpha)$[20] of the Early Church. He never accepted the sharp boundary of rationality between emotion and reason. Here his personal practice was far ahead of his innovative theory.

A main notion for what I call love for the poor was "the privilege of problem formulation" to Frostin.[21] This signifies that already formulating a problem influences the road to the solution and the answer. That is why it is important that the rich do not formulate the problems of the poor, that men do not formulate women's problems, and that the healthy people do not formulate the problems of sick people. The privilege and preference to express experiences of agony must lie with those who are in agony.

Within the Western tradition, it is not quite possible to bring forward such an attitude and approach.

Ever since antiquity, there have been two guiding principles:

- the same knows the same and

- you can only get knowledge of what is similar to you.

Liberation theology's thesis, therefore, signifies a radical break with Western view of knowledge. That which is different, the other, now has other knowledge, which still may be discovered. It may be transmitted and shared. Frostin uses the term others have employed, "a shift of paradigm".

Why is it theologically meaningful to assert that man/woman truly can gain knowledge about other people's experiences and perspectives? Why is it theologically meaningful to assert that the poor have knowledge, which is important for the liberation?

In his paper "Capitalism suffocates love" Frostin gives the following three reasons:

- If there is a wish to create society from the bottom and up instead of the other way, then the knowledge of the poor has to be the starting point. For the church, this implies that "the poor convert the church".[22]

- The knowledge of the poor leads them to "doing theology".[23] Thereby the difference is suspended between, on the one hand, academic theology with the claim to absolute objectivity and, on the other hand, theological practice with so-called subjective prerequisites. In consciousness of its normative function, academic theology reflects the interpretation of Christianity embedded in the context. Pastoral theology originates in the believer's experiences and learns from the insights of academic theology. Both the academic and pastoral theologian side with the suppressed in their different work.

- The knowledge of the poor is needed, on the whole, to be able to discover reality. When standing on the upper side of history one does not see the underside. Therefore, only half of reality is visible. To fully identify oneself with the poor is, therefore, a prerequisite to see reality in a new light.

To Frostin it was ultimately Christ's death on the Cross and the Resurrection, which set the pattern for social knowledge. The way to life leads through death according to the history of suffering. The road of knowledge to the truth, therefore, also leads through identifying with those who suffer.[24] Later, he completed this theology of the Cross and Christology with the thought of the Holy Trinity. God as an absolute Trinitarian communion is the model of social vision and for the diaconia of the church in the social fellowship.[25]

After Frostin's death, a concluding remark is in place. One of my aims with this all too limited sketch is to depict Frostin as a thinker of surprisingly strong Lutheran traditions and equally strong creative and constructive innovator. Frostin tried to give preference to the current situation and to those in it suffering from the powers of darkness. This contextualism which at once is both tradition bound and innovative, according to my view, distinguishes the shaping of his image of God and view on life.[26] His contribution to contextual theology could perhaps be described as "new reformatoric realism".

Contextualism – A New Paradigm?

Does the contextual approach to knowledge as Frostin asserts offer a new paradigm for theology? First, let us look at what is meant by paradigm. Then a number of reasons are given for answering the question positively.

According to Kuhn, the word paradigm has two meanings:[27] i) sociologically a whole constellation of opinions, values, methods etc. shared by members in a given fellowship and ii) philosophically by designating the concrete problem solutions which, used as models or examples, may replace explicit rules as the basis of solutions for "normal" science.

In the first sociological meaning, the contextual approach to knowledge already implies a new paradigm as its basic points are embraced by a large number of male and female scientists including theologians. It is still controversial to what extent the contextual approach to knowledge generally and the contextual theology particularly constitute a shift of paradigm in the second sense.

What reasons are there for letting the contextual approach to knowledge offer new problem solutions, models or examples for systematic theology?

– The contextual approach to knowledge leads theology out of the post-modern dilemma created by the opposition between objectivism and relativism in perspectives on knowledge. Contextuality profits by the method of deconstruction, which criticizes particularity being raised to a universal and normative approach. It offers a possibility of transforming both the objectivism and the relativism in the view of knowledge. The reason being that it stresses knowledge in the local specific context as a necessary prerequisite for each perspective wanting to enter into dialog with other contextual perspectives. For such inter-contextual dialogue, discourse ethics and communication philosophy offer, like non-dogmatic pragmatism, functioning theories with sensible conditions. The contextual approach to knowledge therefore, serves theology's intention to shape its activity as contribution to an inter-contextual and interreligious discourse.

– A contextual approach to knowledge may enter into association with theology's classical paradigm, which united theological rationality, wisdom and an embedding of practice in the fellowship of faith. If one includes a contextual view of knowledge, this also stretches out to the history of theology. The analysis of the context of origin of a theological form of expression gets an important function of the understanding and brings to the fore of interpretations of faith and life from the past.

– Contextual theology differs from a liberal theology, which raises Western rationality to be the yardstick of all the world's views on faith and life. In the challenge to an intercultural and interreligious dialog, the contextual approach to knowledge helps theology both listen to other unknown interpretations of life and express its specific interpretation of life in a Western late modern context.

– The contextual approach to knowledge adds an important function to the producers of theology. It expands and deepens theology's basis in reality and increases its reflexive conditions. It puts academic theology in the position to practically and theoretically develop and differentiate new relations in spheres where Christian spirituality and interpretations of life arise.

– A contextual approach to knowledge may by applied to all the subjects of Religious Studies. There are ongoing experiments with such applications at, for example, the Natal University in South Africa.

– Theology increases its knowledge of the manifold of reality and the potential of conflicts and conflict solutions by awarding the suppressed preference in the theological discourse. Furthermore, it increases its qualifications for constructive contributions, which may actively step into the modernization process.

– Theology's qualifications for interdisciplinary collaboration increase through the attachment to contextuality.

Summary

- A new approach to knowledge is developing. Its growth is ongoing and not completed. This mirrors a reappraisal of the knowledge theories of the age of enlightenment. It concerns the universal theory of the essence of knowledge, which no longer is evidently meaningful and desirable. The transformation of the view on knowledge constitutes a stage in the ongoing progress of social modernization.

- The new approach to knowledge has four characteristics:

  - The question of the subjects of knowledge and their social contexts come to the foreground.

  - Interest in the essence of knowledge is shifted to the question of the social and ecological context and function of knowledge.

  - The importance of method pluralism is stressed. Neither hermeneutics nor empiricism is allowed to become ideologies. Deductive and inductive methods do not confront each other but are linked together in new method developments. Methods for interpreting non-lingual visual expressions become more important.

  - The scientific process of problem formulation becomes to an increasing degree public. Argumentation around the question of why an academic problem is a problem becomes important. Who is touched by the problem? How does the knowledge process constitute a solution to the problem? The perspectives of knowledge from the underside of history and nature are accentuated.

- The new approach to knowledge challenges theology to work with four questions:

  - Which partners in discussions do the actors in academic systematic theology choose and why?

  - Which function belongs to the analysis of context in the theological process of interpretation?

  - How is methodical pluralism within Religious Studies valued?

- How in practical terms does the academic organization satisfy the need for a new orientation around essential problems in our age?

- In his pioneering research the Swedish theologian Per Frostin (1943-1992) made important contributions to meet the epistemological challenge to theology. Frostin's view of the knowledge of theology may be summed up in six criteria:

  - The understanding and the theory of interpretation are put into a political action context (the political hermeneutics).

  - The knowledge of each domain is determined by the context within which it arises. No individual can achieve general and eternal knowledge (the context).

  - The fact that knowledge is determined by specific contexts does not mean that reality is fragmented. Reality and history remain one (the whole).

  - Experiences of conflict, especially, lead to discoveries. There is a clear difference between knowledge from "above" and knowledge from "below". Those who have experiences of the dark side of life perceive reality in a different way than the rich, the powerful and educated people (divergence).

  - The experience of the suppressed in our surrounding world answers to the suppressed experiences within us (identification).

  - The love for the poor is an expression of the love for God and it leads to giving preference to their knowledge.

- There are several reasons for letting the contextual view on knowledge be the new paradigm of theology:

  - A contextual approach to knowledge leads theology out of the postmodern dilemma created by the differences between the objectivist and relativist perspective on knowledge. Theology increases its knowledge of reality's manifold through the experiences of the suppressed and their perspectives.

  - A contextual approach to knowledge may enter in union with theology's classical paradigm, which unites theological rationality, wisdom, and the embedding of practice in the fellowship of faith.

- The interculturally shaped contextual theology overcomes the liberal, Euro-centrist theology, which elevates Western rationality to be the standard for all the world's ideologies.

- It acknowledges that the producers of theology have an important function and thereby deepens theology's firm link with reality.

- A contextual approach to knowledge can be applied to all subjects of Religious Studies. By acknowledging preference to the experiences and perspectives of the suppressed, theology increases its knowledge of reality's manifold and its potential in conflicts and conflict solving.

- Theology's qualifications for interdisciplinary cooperation are augmented by its connection with contextuality.

Notes

[1] Cf. Bernstein, p. 19, p. 81, who ascertains a "movement beyond objectivism and relativism". He discusses, pp. 269–271, Rorty's critique of objectivism as a new relativism.

[2] Cf. Hornborg's essay (1994a) with a foundational argumentation for contextualism's normative epistemology for anthropology and human ecology.

[3] Cf. Shiva, p. 224.

[4] Berger and Luckmann, p. 3.

[5] Tillich, p. 73.

[6] Bergmann and Bråkenhielm (1997).

[7] Sandström (1993), p. 87, pp. 96–98. Cf. Sandström (1995), pp. 23–26.

[8] Maxwell, p. 205.

[9] Maxwell, p. 205.

[10] Maxwell, p. 225.

[11] Bergmann (1994a), pp. 86–88.

[12] Frostin (1988), p. 22.

[13] Frostin (1970), pp. 159–162.

[14] The notion "theology of repristination" means "to copy the solutions of earlier Christian generations without any critical investigation of their relevance today". Frostin (1970), p. 94. The latin "repristinatio" means to throw something into a former condition.

[15] Frostin's political theology should be understood in a larger geographical context. 1971 Dorothee Sölle published in Germany her influential settlement with Bultmann's theology: "Politische Theologie." Frostin's extensive interpretation of Marx was published in German 1978: "Materialismus-Ideologie-Religion."

[16] Cf. Frostin (1992), pp. 27–30. Here he relates to the theory of the "socially constructed ordinary knowledge" in the sociology of knowledge (Berger and Luckmann).

[17]Frostin (1992), p. 32. Cf. also "Kairos Sweden", where Frostin was among the authors.

[18]Frostin (1992), p. 33.

[19]Two years after his death we published Frostin's monograph "The Two Kingdom's Doctrine – A Critical Study" (Studia Theologica Lundensia 48), 1994.

[20]Cf. Gregory of Nazianz' 14. homilia on "The Love of the Poor".

[21]The notion "privilege of problem formulation" was introduced by liberation theologian Hugo Assmann.

[22]Frostin (1985), pp. 34–35.

[23]Frostin (1985), p. 36.

[24]Frostin (1985), pp. 72–73.

[25]See Frostin (1992).

[26]On an international horizon Frostin's work has been located by David Bosch in "Transforming Mission", pp. 423-424, pp. 436–439.

[27]Kuhn, p. 186

Chapter 5

Models of Contextual Theology

Which background theories make a basis for contextual theologies? How is it possible to understand the differences between the diversity of theological approaches? Could a more abstract discussion of contextual theology's different models contribute to solving conflicts and, in this way, create conditions for a future well-integrated model?[1]

In his book "Models of contextual theology", the North American, catholic mission scholar, Stephen B. Bevans, differentiates between five models for contextual theology. For Bevans a theoretical model is something which simplifies a complex reality. The model does not capture all of reality; however, it expresses some knowledge of it. Bevans distinguishes between exclusive, paradigmatic, inclusive, descriptive and complementary models.[2]

In this chapter, I will follow the classification of Bevans into five different models of contextual theology. The classification is preliminary and leaves many open questions open. Rather than offering a conclusive structure, the aim is to create profiles of various approaches and problems. I will characterize each model, and then discuss objections and advantages. Finally, I will propose a sixth, human ecological model.

The Translation Model

According to Bevans, the translation model departs from the assumption that the message of the Gospel is unchangeable and that culture and social patterns of change constitute "vehicles for this essential, unchanging deposit of truth".[3] Bevans mentions Pope John Paul II as representative of this model. The task of theology in this model is a translation of meanings in the Christian learning system into different cultural contexts. In this model, we regard the essential message of Christianity as supra-cultural, i.e. the message content is a "pure Gospel".

The metaphor "the essence", in the meaning of something within, solid and central, is used freely. In spite of the translation model aiming at interpreting the meeting between the Gospel and culture, we give culture an inferior significance and raise the Gospel to be the norm of culture. In this model, the notion of revelation is propositional, that is, revelation is conceived as something the theologian can interpret and explain by the way of several unambiguous statements of faith. According to Bevans, in this model revelation is something radically different from culture.

Like with Warren's patriarchal analysis, we may understand this model as an expression of a dualistic, hierarchic interpretation of reality as its image of the world differs between two "floors". We imagine the world as two separate spheres, i.e. one cultural and one supra-cultural. The task of the translation theologian is to explain the meeting between the two. He is a kind of "messenger" of the Gospel.

In Creation theological terms, this model follows the classical distinction between Creation and Creator even if the distinction here wins such fundamental importance, that it threatens to narrow the theologian's perception of God in function, of the incarnation and of the ongoing revelation mystery.

The communication researcher Marshall MacLuhan once minted the expression that the "form is the message". Interpretation theology disregards this insight and differentiates strictly between form and content and lets the form be only a tool. We may object and ask if translation theology represents modern society's instrumental "goal rationality" (Max Weber) rather than the classical approach to a theological expression. To my eyes, it does not seem as if the Gospel's and the Early Church's theologians acted as if God was absent in their Hellenistic and Jewish cultures.

From the point of view of Creation theology, we may object and ask if translation theology does not in fact reduce the well-created nature and God-like human culture to objects for the theologian to uninhibitedly exploit to the aims of his church.

The Anthropological Model

In the anthropological model, human experience is placed at centre. The theologian makes use of social and cultural anthropological methods. The interpretation of life occurs in close connection with the symbolic conceptualization of an ethnic group's worldview and religion.

Within the framework of this attempt, the notions of inculturation and indigenization have been added. They represent forms of expression of the encounter of Christianity and the earlier non-Christian culture. In the anthropological model, according to Bevans, humankind is viewed as the place of the revelation and a source of theology. Humankind becomes as important as writing and tradition.[4] Revelation occurs in the culture.

Bevans shows how the anthropological model stresses the revelation's importance. The theologian who makes use of anthropology assumes that reality contains a meaning and that the popular extra-European culture shapes and interprets this meaning through its world-view.

In his/her field studies, the anthropologist gives a large share of sympathy to the culture that he/she is studying. The aim of the research is often to contribute in some way to the survival of this culture. The anthropological method is abundant and complex. Among other things, it may consist of language studies which analyze the connections between the interpretation of reality and the language structure; behavioural observations and pragmatic interpretations; and of research into rites which scrutinizes the connections between the outer and inner aspects of the rite and the material, social and mental culture.[5]

Bevans stresses the closeness to reality as being among the positive sides of this model. A theologian working anthropologically treats human life conditions, questions and interests very seriously. From the theological point of view, Bevans judges the revelation in this model to be interpreted as an occurrence in the culture and that the notion of Creation is fully justified. However, Bevans criticizes this model for lack of critical thinking and for its tendency to stoop to "cultural romanticism".[6] He further asks if it is really possible to find a situation where the origins of the Gospel depart from a particular culture.

The critical questions that Bevans poses seem justified. Considering the history of anthropology, I wonder though, if we ought not to revise his objection to the anthropologist being too sympathetic and critical to the culture in question.

While anthropologists in the olden days approached extra-European cultures from an evolutionary and hierarchical point of view, contem-

[handwritten margin note: interplay between the original culture & its subsequent encounter c Christianity]

porary anthropology has discarded this theoretical framework in favour of a more immanent study of that different culture. The goal of the older research was to morphologically categorize the expressions of culture. Today this probably has been compensated by a softer and more manifold hermeneutics where one wishes to interpret what is different and understand the problems, which arise in inter- and trans-cultural encounters.

Anthropological research today not only is devoted to extra-European cultures, but it also studies culture phenomena of the West. It does not seem to be threatened by such cultural exoticism, which raises one culture to become the other's norm. It seems to have developed a sufficiently critical reflexivity to send off the older, exploiting ethnography to the archives.[7]

Bevans' second objection is aimed more towards the theologians than towards the anthropologists. If, like Bevans, we ask for a situation where the Gospel truly emanates from a particular culture, then we may naturally only answer that this situation existed in Palestine around the time of Christ's earthly activities.

It seems here as if Bevans falls victim to his own dialectical tool of analysis in which "Gospel" and "culture" are the two poles between which theology mediates. What does Bevans really mean by "Gospel"?

His way of thinking seems absurd if he aims at the concrete collection of texts. A text emanates in one context not in several. On the other hand, if he refers to the Gospel in a more Lutheran sense, meaning the interpretation of life, which we preach, receive and live believing in Christ, then this issue is different.

Already the Reformers assumed that the Gospel in this sense without doubt could work also in other realities than the Palestinian one. God the Creator acted through the Resurrected as the Saviour, and the belief in this God justified the independence of all-contextual characteristics and positions. The christology of Luther leads us, exactly because of this common view of Christ and the context, to such a pioneering view of humans as through the eyes and hands of the painter Matthias Grünewald, which even gives birth to a new attitude towards pictures, that is, Realism.

If the contents of the Gospel mean that God acts, liberates and justifies those who believe here and now, then I wonder if Bevans' distinction between the Gospel and culture does not also lead to a distinction between the doctrine of Salvation and Creation. This would be difficult to associate with either the classical or the reformed tradition.

It would be wrong to over-interpret the reformatory distinctions between Law and Gospel and between the spiritual and the worldly, just as it would be wrong to make the Gospel into the antithesis of culture. Bevans' dialectics tend to oversee the integration aimed at by contextual theologians.

The concept formation inculturation and contextualization grammatically constitute verb constructions. There is deeper sense in expressing the contextual theology's cause not through nouns or adjectives but through verb constructions and prepositions. God inculturates Him/Herself in a people's world: the Son and the Holy Spirit contextualize themselves and become flesh dwelling in different created beings in unique situations for the sake of the world. To contextual theology, God is God in function.

The Praxis Model

The praxis notion is central in Western social theory. Within theology, this notion has been developed above all in Latin American liberation theology and in European political theology . Theology's aim is to make this model a contribution to the change of praxis and, especially, to the liberation of the suppressed groups. Summing up, the method may be described as a critical theological reflection on praxis as a normative contribution to its change.

Among the positive characteristics of the model, Bevans highlights its methodical and epistemological characteristics.[8] The method "see–interpret–act" is well suited to understand the social interplay between experiences, reflections and acts. This method keeps practice and theory apart when at the same time linking both to each other. This model uses the insight that each kind of knowledge is socially determined and, that different groups develop different interpretations of reality and patterns of rationality.

Bevans further emphasizes liberation theology's meritorious interpretation of the revelation and he is of the view that this is in accordance with the approach of classical theology.

The criticism that Bevans advances is known. Liberation theology tends to dissolve the line between Marxist ideology and Christian faith, and it pays too much attention to the signification of conflict for the interpretation of life.

The two objections are possible to meet. In Latin America, liberation theologians consider that the interpretation of their theology as Marxism misreads the function of social theory in the theological system. While in the history of Europe, Marxist theory's conversion to a Stalinist-Leninist ideology of dictatorships has been experienced, the conception of socialism's meaning has another design outside of Europe.

ा liberation theology, Marxist theory of economics works as a theory
ent and not as a leading philosophy which is the case, for example,
istoric materialism. For this reason, we must also differentiate in
the interpretation of divergences between the armed combat of Marxists
and the non-violence commitment of base groups.[9]

Another question to liberation theology concerns the notion of praxis. What is really the theologian's idea of praxis? May we assume
unambiguous interpretations? How do we handle the insight of reality's
complexity in a daily situation where all natural and social science's
"theories about everything" have lost their credibility?[10]

How do we shape a practical theological realism if we do not want
to represent a kind of metaphysical realism, which would be remote to
the liberation theologians?[11]

In Europe during the 16th and 17th centuries, the Reformers also
fought against the ontological straightjacket of Aristotle's scholasticism
that was forced upon the body of theology. They partly succeeded
in tearing a hole in the jacket aided by a soteriological dynamization
of God's image and the view of the human person, but they kept the
ontology inherited from antiquity in relation to the conception of morals
and Creation.

Could one possibly understand the Latin American liberation theology by analogy with the European reformation? The propagation
of Bible reading, the doctrine of salvation and the liberation theme's
structuring importance, as well as the discussion on justice, the debates
on and the relevance of theology might indicate this.

The Correlation Model

Bevans calls a fourth model of contextual theology "the synthetic model". This model aims at balancing the insights of the past three models
and trying to find a middle course.

In his diagram on the polarity between Gospel and culture, Bevans
localizes the translation model on the side of the Gospel and the anthropological model and the praxis model on the side of culture. The
synthetic model, logically, ends up midway between the two poles.

Bevans refers to Schreiter and emphasizes the importance of dialogue in this model. Four variables stand in a mutual relationship to
each other and between all of these an ongoing reciprocal action is in
progress:

   – Gospel/tradition,

– other modes of thinking/cultures,

– culture and

– social change.[12]

According to Bevans, the distinctive feature of this model is the accentuation on openness, pluralism and dialogue. Bevans cites Tracy and his correlation method as a representative for the model, which according to him, best denotes "the true universality of Christian faith".[13]

Since Bevans equates Tracy's correlation theology and his own synthetic model and since he excludes the transcendental model in his synthesis, I prefer to denote Bevans synthetic model as "correlation model".

Among the positive traits of the model, Bevans emphasizes its focus on the aspects of culture communication and its usefulness for local church leaders. Among the negative traits of the model, he criticizes its tendency to oversee the imbalance in power relations between the cultures and its all too vague notion of communications, which threaten to undermine the culture encounter to wishy-washy. On the other hand, Bevans stresses the necessary understanding of differences between the cultures.

In the third chapter we have discussed the deficiencies of correlation theology in relation to a constructive interpretation of tradition. On this point, Bevans seems to take the same stance as Tracy when he asserts that the synthetic model is perhaps best suited to express "the true universality of the Christian faith".

Which criteria are available for judging if the universality is true or false? Does Bevans mean that the reception, that is the communicative survival of a way of thinking and its contents in itself is a guarantor for the faith interpretation's universal truth? If that is the case, he leaves the idea of contextual theology which we sketched in the previous chapter and falls back on the same propositional, objectivist approach to knowledge that he himself criticized.[14]

Might Bevans hold that contextual theology's manifold is a necessary prerequisite for asserting anything about the universality of the Christian faith, that is, about the unity between Creation and Salvation experiences? In that case I readily agree while admitting that contextual theory shaping has not yet developed satisfactory valid arguments for the manifold as a necessary prerequisite for unity.

This observation leads us into one of the most difficult problem areas at the moment in our field. Let us pose two questions:

How could one make contextualism generally applicable without resorting to an objectivist understanding? Under which conditions could contextually modelled insights of knowledge be universal for communicative acts in a global cultural encounter?

The Transcendental Model

Bevans' fifth model is shaped within the frame of transcendental philosophy dating back to Immanuel Kant which, since then has constituted a leading theory for the view of knowledge in the West. This theory does not emanate from the question of knowledge's essence or nature, but it begins with the assumption that something exists which precedes the knowledge of man/woman. When he/she understands, he/she experiences what is in the world and within him/her.

This model has four characteristics. Firstly, the contextual theology, which uses this model, is less interested in the question of how to shape a particular theology. On the other hand, it is interested in the subject producing theology. What is an authentic religious experience? How can I express my faith in culture? How and why can I judge and understand theological work?

Secondly, the transcendentally shaped theology is not exclusively private and subjective. On the contrary, it may also interpret such which is common to several subjects in a cultural fellowship precisely because of its concentration on the authentic, subjective experience.

A third characteristic concerns the revelation. Revelation in this model is not something which takes place "out there", but it takes place in the subjective experience which a human being makes out of the world around. Thereby theology only becomes possible for the person who converts and believes. God is revealed in the experience of God. This model says no more about the Creation than that it constitutes the possible prerequisite for the experience and reflection of the subject.[15]

A fourth trait in this model is the assumption that human reason in spite of all culturally and historically conditioned differences functions in a similar way with all subjects at all times and in all places. Transcendental philosophy's doctrine about the existence presupposes some kind of existence of a universal reason. We may supplement Bevans' criticism on this point with the historical observation that the ontology of Kant therewith appears to be marred by the imperfections of Plato's universal soul.

Bevans stresses the power of the transcendental model to focus on the importance of the subject for theology and on the importance of communications between the subject and the other. He objects that one might understand transcendental philosophy as too abstract an outlook, and he asks further if the acceptance of a universal reason might express a particularistic approach.

It seems that the transcendental philosopher is a product of the Western, male-centred culture. We can ask how he deals with the occurrence of different forms of knowledge and different methods for attaining insights of truth.

Bevans' criticism seems well founded when concerning the older, so-called neo-Kantian, approach to knowledge. One might add that it was, in addition, closely associated with Newton's worldview of physical order and, therefore, to a high degree pays attention to the similarity between material and subjective structures without grasping evolutionary transformation phenomena.

In his criticism, however, Bevans entirely oversees the fact that Kant's philosophy still today distinguishes itself through a vital continuity. Its tradition is far from being over, and the critical and transcendental approach to knowledge creates important contributions to social theory in Europe and in the United States. The social philosophers of the Frankfurter School, Jürgen Habermas and Karl-Otto Apel, work in this tradition, and they have managed to develop a convincing synthesis of the pragmatism and the older transcendental philosophy. The background theory for the interpretation of society, which was developed by Habermas and Apel, has successfully created conditions for a fruitful dialogue between North American and Western European intellectuals. This outlook on society unfortunately tends to blind the experiences outside the West and the ecological theory perspectives.[16]

To sum up, we will illuminate yet another model to further the demand for shaping a synthetic model. This would take care of both the subject insights of transcendental philosophy and the other model insights in society, culture and history.

A Human Ecological Model

Unlike the five models which theologians have already developed the human ecological model consists of an outline and proposal. I allow myself to experiment a little and try the different theories' relevance to theology.

The human ecological model links up with several insights in the models described so far. The criticism against the translation model and the theology of the eternity remains. I will be using an anthropologically developed notion of religion in a prolongation of the anthropologic model. The central theme of liberation of the praxis model is preserved at the same time as its praxis notion is differentiated so that reality appears both in its complexity and integrity. The correlation model's focus on the problem of communication becomes a central problem also in the human ecological model, which nevertheless prefers an action theory notion of communication rather than an idealistic notion. Transcendental philosophy contributes to the human ecological model by paying attention to the signification of subjectivity and unity.

In this way, the human ecological model consists of a synthesis of the preceding models with the exception of the translation model. This is however, not merely a combination but it accentuates what the other models overlook, in other words the signification of the Creator, the place and the physical world for theology.

What do we understand by human ecology?

Human Ecology and Religion

Human ecology partly treats questions of survival, especially human exploitation of nature resources, partly questions concerning the history of relations to nature and partly questions concerned with "how ideas intervene into material processes, how material reality is literally shaped by our image of it, by our symbol system and by the meaning we gather from them".[17]

The Swedish social anthropologist and human ecologist, Alf Hornborg, relates the notions of truth and survival to each other, so that the truth value of one alternative system of ideas simply mirrors a higher life value.[18] He characterizes the normative aim of human ecology as work with the questions of how a sensible comprehensive view may be regained, how the world of notions may be changed so that the rational coincides with survival, and how reason may create more space for the sacral.

With orientation towards a semiotic theory, Hornborg advances the thesis that local knowledge, for instance among indigenous populations, ought not to be drained as a resource but that ecological anthropology should devote itself to the social cultural contexts in which ecologically sensitive knowledge systems may develop and endure in time.[19]

In a case study, Hornborg applies the human ecological theory on the understanding of the Canadian Mi'kmaq environmental engagement to preserve their holy mountain being threatened by industrial mining and financial interests.[20] Hornborg explains the behaviour of the Mi'kmaq as a striving for specific physical and spiritual, local expressions in the light of the theory of modernity's processes of decontextualization and universal encirclement.

Hornborg characterizes the importance of the place in anthropological contexts as a tendency to "resurrection" of the place and, in my book "Geist, der Natur befreit," I have stressed the importance of place to a trinitarian and pneumatological shaping of Creation theology. This was done by the help of the biblical and the Early Churches' notion of "the place where the Holy Spirit takes its dwelling."

Where is the significance of religion and Christian theology for human ecology? Religion, images of God, experiences and conceptions of what is holy are all about things that are inaccessible to humans.[21] Similarly we may define nature in its entirety constantly withdrawing from humans and at the same time responding to advances. The image of God may be said to win importance and function in the mediation between the worldview and ethos, between the understanding of humanity and people's intermediate praxis and between man's view of nature and his/her behaviour in and use of nature.[22] The lack or reduction of religious attitudes and values also has a function in this interplay.

Independently of which approach to religion one stands for, it seems meaningful to include the question of the function of religion in treating the problems of human relations to nature. To put it simply, what is it that functions as "god" in the understanding of humans in nature and their praxis in and with it? What do different environmental agents attach their heart to? Which God is in function when humans act like the keepers or vandals of nature?

One of several reasons to integrate human ecology and theology is that theology's issue of God makes it possible to constantly keep the ideologically-critical question alive without which human ecology would congeal and crystallize. Owing to the question of what functions as God, one lessens the risk of the conservationist movement and its reflection falling victim to a threatening ideological biologism and for the naturalization of social problems which creates more problems than it solves.[23] According to Hermann Daly and John B. Cobb, the monist notion of God even offers a "guarantee against idolatry".[24]

An ideologically unenlightened, cheap normativity falls back on the notion figure: what seems natural – through our eyes – is good, and what is good ought to be done. In other words, what seems good through our eyes ought to be done.

On the other hand, a precious normativity contains a critical scrutiny of magic formula like the one that all environmental problems may be solved through self-redeeming technical automats, whether they are new metaphores, new technology or new system knowledge. The precious normativity is only won in the interplay between three links: experience of conflict, intuitive and discursive interpretation, and experimental trouble-shooting the significance of which is created by all those affected by the conflict. In this connection, a human ecologically shaped theology could contribute to a normative peace and conflict research in the field of conflict between humans and nature.

Human ecology in the sight of God keeps all its concentration on the connection between human and nature systems while keeping its horizon open for the necessary task of crossing over systems and borders. By including the question of God in its activity, human ecology wins a science transforming, "trans-scientific"[25] but also "trans-cultural" potential.[26]

Which human ecological theories could become relevant for contextual theology?

God in Function in the Surrounding World

The biologist Jakob von Uexküll has developed the theory of the "circle of function" in his zoological behavioural research. To von Uexküll all living organisms are subjects, and according to him the "surrounding world" of the subjects and their "inner world" consists of an "acting world" (Wirkwelt) and a "perception world" (Merkwelt).[27] These two worlds interact with each other in a circular motion. The different organisms' circles of acting and perception have different characteristics and their perspectives on the common surroundings intersect. In 1935 von Uexküll invents the notion "Umwelt" to designate the environment common to the different organisms.

von Uexküll's model is possible to work out as a human ecological interpretation model. In this outlook on nature through perception, experience and thinking interacts with relations to nature in many acts.

A human ecological model for theology implies that the help of this circle of function reflects human experience and interpretation of the acting God.

God acts in nature, is perceived through human senses in the world of action and is interpreted in the worlds of reason and perception. Traditions, cultural patterns and language, all offer tools for the perception and interpretation. In this model, the theologian interprets the experience of God likewise aesthetically and rationally.

Perception in its turn interacts through the human bodily acts with the other subject's worlds of action. Culturally and historically coded experiences and memories are expressed in the form of prayers, texts, the building of churches and welfare work.

The human ecological model assumes that people's worlds of perception and action intersect and that agents in fellowship exchange expressions with the help of intersubjective sign systems such as bodily, figurative, linguistic or musical sign systems. The revelation takes place and is interpreted theologically in this semiotic and communicative space.

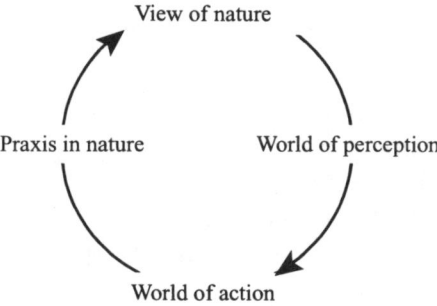

Figure 5.1: The human ecological circle of function

Ecological Liberation Theology

Unlike Bevans, in the human ecological model I do not presuppose that there is polarity between Gospel and culture, but I use the word "gospel" to designate answers to God's acting. Gospel is at the same time a tiding about God's acting and an answer to this. It is a form of expression of the belief that the Son and the Holy Spirit act visibly in nature and in culture.

Thereby it becomes possible to shape the human ecological model by the help of the thought of the circle of function. Theology interprets God in function, the God that through a liberating movement "circles" between perception and cooperation with those created. God's existence and God's liberating, ontology and soteriology, are thus no longer in an opposing relation. The task of theology in this model is to interpret the Saviour's liberating movement and interpret God to the world.

In the human ecological model, contextual theology overrules the axiom that nature is revelation's and morality's prerequisite a priori and ontologically. The existence of Creation does not need to be guarantor for Salvation or the proof of theology to existence of the Creator.

Creation is in this theology understood instead as an object for and a partner of God's love. As such, everything created becomes part not only of human sighs and anguish but also of liberation. Human ecological theology widens liberation theology to comprise natural history. The main task of ecological liberation theology is, therefore, to answer the question of the surrounding worlds, organisms and humans: God, why did you create us and why and into what are you liberating us?[28]

He became like us that we may become like him.

Christian Faith and Religion

A third characteristic in the human ecological model is its positive use of the notion of religion and ideology.

While for instance Karl Barth during the 1940s asserted a divergence between religion and Christianity, one could hardly adhere to this in the contemporary situation of ideological and religious pluralism. Perhaps this distinction was strategically justified in Barth's historical situation where strong powers melted together ancient Norse religious elements and Christianity to a nazi Blut-und-Boden devotion in contrast to the supposed Jewish idolatry. The assertion that Christianity alone was capable of offering criteria to judge what was the Word of the Lord became questioned even by the contemporaries of Barth.

Theologians in the Barth tradition today do not adhere to this aspect of his production, but some emphasize him as a contextual theologian.[29] Some scholars even assert that he in his accentuating of God forestalled the postmodernist view on linguistics.

The latter thesis seems rather far-fetched, as Barth in his approach to knowledge evidently was impressed by the contemporary view on objectivist confidence in the possibility of positive knowledge. The theology of Barth was altogether based on kerygma, which does not problemize the question of criteria for the Gospel interpretation to a sufficiently high degree to become contextual.

Of more interest, however, is his partly successful intention, through the theology of Creation and revelation to shield the Christian interpretation of life against the contemporary age's successfully organized idolatry.

Today we are possibly slightly wiser due to the experiences of religiously legitimate anti-Semitism and a racist outlook on humans during the first half of the last century. The dialogue of religion and culture is not only the business of social leaders, but it is also relevant for many citizens in everyday urban places. A challenge is created by the political and economic patterns of mobility and immigration caused by factors during the 1990s in Europe and this results in increasingly urgent problems. In this situation it seems totally unreasonable to uphold a partition between Christian faith and religion.

A further challenge to interpreting Christian faith as "religion" is the growth of a multitude of new interpretations of spiritual life. These partly develop an emancipating and partly a spiritualizing relevance.[30] Theologically, a partition of Christian faith from other expressions of faith today could lead to the Christian idea of Creation being pushed into the margin. When in a public discussion it is no longer possible to make credible the faith in Creation and the view on the human person as the image of God, then it will also be impossible to attain social credibility for the thought of Christ's and the Holy Spirit's ongoing history of redemption.

There is therefore, good reason to examine if anthropological studies notion of religion might offer support to the human ecological model. Anthropologists shaped their understanding of religion to be able to treat many different cultures with a unified frame of theories. Their notion of religion thus tends to become slightly too diffuse. However, according to my point of view, it is eminently suited for a specification within contextual theology.

Pragmatics of Religion

The North American anthropologist, Clifford Geertz, in his religion ethnology interprets religion as a "mutual corroboration of worldview and ethos".[31] According to his view, religion not only mirrors the social order of culture but it also shapes culture. To Geertz, ethos signifies a people's way of life. The people's ethos may on the one hand become credible through a worldview, and on the other hand the worldview itself may become credible through the people's ethos. They confirm each other mutually.

Geertz links up to the social theory of Habermas and develops his double structure as follows: In the theory of communicative action, communication consists of the two elements "performative competence", i.e. the capability of forwarding and conveying a message, and a "propositional content". Geertz shapes a model according to which the human social reality is constituted through the symbolic representation according to the double structure of a rational worldview and social acts.

Helped by this outlook, contextual theology and theology of religion can make a pragmatic turn.[32] The signification of religious interpretations and acts, according to this religion-pragmatic theory, may no longer be reduced to the meaning in a subjective experience of transcendence. Religion-pragmatical contextual theory does not exclusively reflect upon the religious intentions of the person, as with Schleiermacher, but contemplates these within a wider horizon. In this model, the approach to human individuality is not restricted to the self of "man".[33] The theologian instead understands humans in this model as something that adds to and acts within a large net of ecological, social and culturally defined relations.

The human ecological model concurs in the pragmatic background theory and thus becomes capable of interpreting the theologically active person in several spheres. While the text-fixed theology studies theologians as authors of books, pragmatics of religion reflect upon the question of how people in different media and circumstances of action express their religious interpretation of life. What functions as God for individuals and groups in different situations? How does a late modern, urbanized, nature religiosity, such as the culture of composting, express itself?[34] Due to the pragmatics of religion, it is possible to interpret expressions not only of church culture but also of youth, work, leisure time and everyday culture.[35]

Helped by this perspective we can understand why Christian faith has been of comparatively little importance for the process of modernization. A belief in God could hardly regulate for instance the industrialization of the natural sciences as this underlying worldview was diametrically opposing the basic traits in the belief in God. The approach to man/woman as an economic creature, homo oeconomicus, was inconsistent with the Jewish-Christian view on the human person as the image of God.[36] The view of nature as a gift and Creation was incompatible with the modern view of nature as a resource for human use.[37]

In spite of all so-called secularization, we may wonder if the Christian faith in God in combination with more diffuse religious fragments has been in function in an unobtrusive manner during the 20th century. Examples include private religiosity and popular usage.

Statistical studies in Sweden in connection with the Estonia catastrophe, in 1995, show that religion and the church have fulfilled important functions for the expressions of grieving and anguish of a large number of citizens.[38] To some extent, the Christian churches were able to organize this faith even if it sometimes happened in a spirit of steering from above and therapeutically. The churches were not, on the other hand, able to reflect upon the fact that the accident also may be understood in the light of qualitative high risk-taking in a modern technological society. Only technicians and journalists were able to formulate the question of the value of human life in the income-bringing business of ferry technology at sea.

Pragmatics of religion ought to be, in similar situations, an important partner for contextual theology as the empirically and statistically working sociology of religion merely is capable of quantitatively describing practical religious expressions. During the last few years, the objectives of sociologists of religion have to a lesser extent been complex behaviour in the field but mainly the statistically constructed basis of selected decision problems. Pragmatics of religion, on the other hand, may offer qualitative interpretations including both empirical and hermeneutical aspects in union with contextual theology's reflection on the question of God.

Theology's Physical Surroundings

The human ecological model further attaches independent importance to the physical dimension of context. Human ecology develops in Sweden as a scientific reflection on the human pattern of support and its interaction with the understanding of nature and the human practice in it.

If we apply such a perspective on theology, the question arises how the physical factors of the surrounding world interact with the shaping of theology. This perspective is not to be misunderstood as a materialistic philosophy. The merit of human ecology lies in surmounting the old antagonism between idealism and materialism. The focus of a human ecological perspective ends up the interaction between materia and idea not the contradiction of them.

The historian Carolyn Merchant offers a well-differentiated model of interplay between physical, economic, ethical, conceptual and symbolic aspects of reality. She assumes that there is a basic connection between spiritual and physical patterns of production and reproduction, and she successfully interprets the modernization of the American region of New England between 1750 and 1950 by the help of her theory.

The human ecological model of contextual theology along with Merchant's theory is able to perceive religion both as a product of and a contribution to continuity and the transformation of social and ecological life cycles.

For pastoral theology, on the other hand, there arises the possibility of developing theological perspectives on the support system, economic responsibilities and political behaviour of a county or a parish. The conception of reality does not disintegrate into physical, social and supra-worldly part with such point of view, but the local landscape and fellowship picture can be held together with the help of the human ecological conception of reality.

The demand for an increased integration of physical, social and cultural, as well as religious aspects is not as radical as it may seem. Members of the environmental movement, who at least rhetorically constitute a majority of the population in the West, seem to have recognized this demand. Environmentalists often talk about the need for a spiritual deepening for the environmental struggle to succeed peacefully.[39]

As regards the various nominations, there appears in this situation the challenge of meeting the growing sympathy for the environment and the new spiritualism. Theology is challenged to creatively interpret the liberating revelation of God amidst those engaged in environmentalism.[40] The reflection on the significance of the rite is an important element in the theological answer to the questions of human ecology.

The American anthropologist Roy R. Rappaport has shown how the religious rite among the people of New Guinea is closely tied to nature relations and their culturally coherent approach to nature. In that way, the rite contributes to regulating nature relations and certain ritual element lead to the ecosystem being protected against over-exploitation.[41] We may ask ourselves which traditions in the Christian religion are suited for developing similar regulating mechanisms.

The "Day of the Earth" is celebrated as a national holiday in the United States since 20 April 1970. The theologian Jürgen Moltmann has in his theology of Creation called attention to the thought that the goal of Creation is the Sabbath. How could we interpret in an ecotheological way the importance of the day of rest? How does one today reconstruct the Christian tradition in which the early Christians once a week celebrated liturgies of resurrection?

In the light of the ecological challenge, could a practical contextual theology, for example, plead for liturgies for "the resurrection of Creation" and to "the memory of extinct species"?[42] How can we interpret the compost on the cemetery and in the villa garden as a practical physical expression of the belief that God loves and looks after the Earth and the living?

In the human ecological model contextual theology emphasizes not only the social and environmental ethical question. Here the theologian goes one step further and even tries to legitimize practical patterns of behaviour in the form of rites and thoughts, which may permeate life styles. In this way, contextual theology develops a different normativity than the one, which in accordance with the tradition of natural law separates dogma from ethics so that the former constitutes the latter's foundation.

In the human ecological model, ethics is not that which follows dogma. The good deeds are not simply construed as fruits of faith. On the other hand, a human ecological theology emphasizes the mutuality between the conception of moral and the image of God, between deeds and faith.

Contextual theology is in this sense practical and theoretical aesthetics, i.e. a reflection upon the conditions and possibilities of perception and shaping. Experiments, creative examinations and games are, for this reason, indispensable methodical tools for the creation of the human ecological Christian approach to life. In the centre of this experiment stands the question of how theology may contribute to the worldview and ethos of that which is created in common surroundings may provide mutual support so as to promote everyone's survival?

It is necessary to meet the challenge to a creative new translation of human ecological interpretation of God today to avoid a flight from reality and the adversities of the environmental struggle, which might be caused by the new spirituality growing in the environmental movement. It is natural that Christian theology alone cannot lay claim to explaining the growth of the new nature spirituality.

In the older and younger religions, it is of importance that the faithful can meet each other in a mutual, practical and theoretical discourse. This would centre on the contributions of religion to the solving of survival problems.

A reconstruction of Christian theology would probably not be sufficient in this situation, as such attempts tend to be apologetic and defensive. As I see it, only a creative new construction of theology's interpretation of traditions and situations may lead to convincing answers to totally new questions in an earlier unknown state of society.

Thus the human ecological model goes over and above the claims of the correlation model asserting that it is not possible, as Paul Tillich

claims, to assume that Christian tradition in itself contains the answers
to the questions posed by the situation.

In the expressions of Christian faith, content and form will always
be inseparably woven together. If a cultural form of expression changes
shape its content is also transformed even if the inner transformation
proceeds a good deal slower. In a new situation, therefore, not only the
question but also the answer changes.

In human ecology's Christian image of God, accordingly God becomes a God who tends and promotes the survival of sensitive cultural
and ecological systems where the very foundation of existence is threatened by an unjust "world system" (Immanuel Wallerstein). The theologian grasps revelation in this model as an ongoing development in which
God protects the manifold and development in nature and culture. God
the Creator saves through the Son the fellowship of the living from evil.
Through the Holy Spirit He gives life to the world to come.

Summary

There are six characteristics in this sketch of a human ecological model
for contextual theology:

- God's revelation is translated as a liberating act in the circle of
  function between the human view of nature and her practice in
  it. God's Holy Spirit gives life and perfects nature, culture and
  humanity. Contextual theology reflects on the acting of God in
  the manifold of the living people's perspectives, which intersect
  in a common environment.

- The central question for ecological liberation theology is how the
  Creator preserves and liberates from evil the life fellowships of
  those created.

- The human ecological model uses a functional notion of religion,
  which seeks religion in the interaction between image of the worldview and ethos. Theology qualifies anthropology with special consideration of the Christian experience of God and expression of
  God's image. The background theory of pragmatics of religion
  creates new conditions for a human ecologically conscious, intra-
  cultural and intra-religious reflection on the problems in nature
  relations.

- In the human ecological model, religion and the Christian belief in
  God is understood as part of a complex context of physical, social

and conceptual production and reproduction patterns. Theology thereby is not reduced to a materialistic equation but highlights both the dependence on material and social factors and their specific ability to intervene and change these.

- The object of contextual theology in this model is God in function in social ecological situations and places. The prayer, the rite, the text and everyday life make up important sources and tools for the growth of this theology.

Due to the ecologically anthropologically inspired approach to religion, contextual theology changes its moral philosophical background of theory. The notion of this ethics is not only moral actions as products of faith or an objective stoic construction of the natural moral law. There are two questions in the centre of contextual ethics: How do the experiences of God and their expressions interact with moral deeds? How is the Christian image of God able to regulate the interaction between the worldview and ethos?

- Contextual theology contributes to the human ecological model by a thorough new interpretation of revelation treating it with special consideration of the spirituality in the environmental movement. In contrast to the correlation model, it safeguards against the possibility of earlier unknown and as yet untried Christian interpretations of life. In that way it contributes to Christianity's continuity and its renewal in a variable culture.

To express it briefly: contextual theology is shaped in the human ecological model ecologically and semiotically, soteriologically, religion anthropologically and dynamically, social ecologically and normatively as well as being pneumatologically and creatively conscious of traditions.

Remaining to be developed in the future, is the question how this human ecological model gets its social shape in the church. Individual believers, Christian parishes and church leaders have shown great ability to take responsibility for the foreign fellow-creatures in our midst. This realized human ecological model offers notions and patterns of thought, which can help the baptized people in different denominations to a similar perspective and take responsibility for those "foreign" forms of life which by Creation theologically constitute our "siblings". Applied, it expresses a transformed view of "the sun, my father" and "the earth, our mother" (Nils Aslak Valkeapää), on the landscape as the face of God and on the interplay between the different forms of life as a "cosmic democracy" (Leonardo Boff). The human ecological challenge of the church is creating a blend of new and old songs of praise, artistically carefully shaping global and local responsibility taking nature as a creation without making humans the measure of everything.

Quite a few problems are unsolved, even if the human ecological model through its union of the many aspects makes a synthesis of the above-mentioned models.

Such a problem concerns the aesthetic dimension. The term aesthetics here means partly perception of the senses and partly formation.[43] In the connection of fellow humans and ecology the reflection plays an important role. The reflection and the linguistic rational handling of reality only consist of one among several human aptitudes. Sensuality and non-verbal forms of expression are other and perhaps more important aspects. As we saw, the art historian Sven Sandström, showed how "thinking in images" even makes a necessary prerequisite for verbal communication and discursive thinking.

A human ecological model for contextual theology is, therefore, in need of a reflection upon the aesthetic interaction between nature, the subject and culture and its signification for theology.

How does the perception of a development and a space in landscape affect thinking, and how does a sensual way of thinking influence the acting in and the shaping of the same space in landscape? How does experience of the senses influence the interpretation of God's revelation?[44] In which way do we express an experience, a feeling or a thought within other aesthetic media than words?

One way of working on these types of questions is an inter-disciplinary co-operation for example between theology, physiology, psychology and technical sciences. Another way is to develop contextual pedagogics, for example with a basis of the "pedagogics for the suppressed" by the Brazilian philosopher Paulo Freire. A third way is approaching aesthetics through the visual arts. In the concluding Chapter I choose the latter way and ask what significance the artist's image creating and creativity may win for contextual theology.

Notes

[1] Also Sallie McFague, p. 41, p. 66, departs in her latest book from the thesis of this book, i.e. that all theology is contextual. My criticism of McFague's approach focusses on (a) her still idealistic dependence seeking for "a Christian theology of the good life" (xiii) which means the quest for one theology for one good life, (b) her problematic subordination of the Son under the Father (Cf. pp. 19–20.), (c) her tendency to a "theologia regenitorum", i.e. to articulate a confession meaningful only for Christian re-born believers, and (d) her ethical belief that the change of metaphors in itself changes our view and usage of nature. For a more explicit discussion with McFague see Bergmann (1995a), pp. 243, 251, 267, 275, 283, 288, 304 and 311.

[2] Bevans, p. 26.

[3] Bevans, p. 31. Cf. also my criticism of the Creation theology of the German lutheran theologian Oswald Bayer who understands the task of theology as "an activity of translation", in: Bergmann (1995a), pp. 71–72.

[4] Bevans, p. 48.

[5] In its own research history the discipline of anthropology is characterized by a dialectics or a confrontation of hermeneutical and structuralistic conceptions. Significant for anthropology today is, according to Århem, p. 25, the researcher's change between participation and reflection and anthropology's holistic search for an understanding of connections between different phenomenas.

[6] Bevans, p. 53.

[7] Århem, pp. 18–20.

[8] Bevans, pp. 70–71.

[9] Cf. Hofmann, pp. 53–54.

[10] At the same time as the conditions for "a theory of everything" are destroyed we also can register an increasing interest to construct new cosmologies. On the notion of "cosmology", its history and reconstruction see the entry "Kosmologie" in: Historisches Wörterbuch der Philosophie 4, 1153-1155.

[11] In spite of his strong intention and capacity to articulate perspectives of high relevance for practice, the famous Brazilian liberation theologian Leonardo Boff does not succeed with a consequential ontological realism, but recurs in his social ethics to the axiom of the natural law. Cf. my critical discussion of Boff's sociomorphism in Bergmann (1995a), pp. 327–328.

[12] Bevans, p. 86.

[13] Bevans, p. 87.

[14] One might be able to solve this dilemma through a semiotic understanding of truth which was undertaken by Schreiter. Bevans does not try this method and I am not so sure about its possibilities.

[15] Against Picht, who with strong reasons interprets Kant as a "philosopher of religion", I would like to claim that Kant's transcendental philosophy lost its Creation-theological potential because of its uncritical reception of Newton's physics. Cf. my positive evaluation of the capacity of transcendental philosophy to emphasize – in analogy to the Eastern patristic apophatic theology – the subject's insight in the limits of knowledge as a necessary condition for truth-insights in general, Bergmann (1995a), pp. 374–377.

[16] This criticism has been developed convincingly by Dussel who since 1991 has discussed with Apel about the intercultural philosophy of dialogue. Only a few theologians, as e.g. Arens, have integrated the social theory of communicative action. A majority prefers to combine empirical (materialistic) analysis of data with (idealistic) historical interpretation in the frame of objectivism.

[17] Hornborg (1992), p. 14.

[18] Hornborg (1992), p. 14.

[19] Hornborg (1994a), p. 13. Regarding Jakob von Uexküll's and Thure von Uexküll's life semiotics see Bergmann (1995a), Chapter V.2.3.3.

[20] Hornborg (1994b).

[21] Cf. Huppenbauer, p. 103.

[22] Cf. Bergmann (1995b), p. 43.

[23] Cf. Beck (1993), pp. 99–148.

[24]Daly and Cobb, p. 401.

[25]Steiner, pp. 49–51.

[26]Regarding the concept of "transculturality" versus monocultural and multicultural theories see Bergmann (2002b).

[27]von Uexküll and Kriszat, p. 11.

[28]Cf. Bergmann (1995a), p. 328.

[29]The German protestant theologian Berthold Klappert offers in his book a consequential contextual interpretation of Karl Barth's theology.

[30]Cf. Pétursson, pp. 82–84.

[31]Geertz, pp. 87–125.

[32]Kippenberg, pp. 45–46. The approach of a pragmatics of religion includes also a criticism of the phenomenology of religion.

[33]The individualistic one-dimensioning of the modern view of man needs to be widened so that men and women are understood as partakers in ecological communities, which is explicitly highlighted in recent feminist approaches of an "ethics of flourishing", e.g. in Cuomo, Chapter III.

[34]Bergmann (1996c).

[35]Kippenberg, p. 60.

[36]Cf. Frostin (1992), pp. 32–33.

[37]Cf. Evernden, pp. 11–48, on the thinking of resource and the commodification in the modern view of nature, even in the environmental movement.

[38]Gustafsson, p. 40.

[39]Recently Anne Primavesi, p. 99, has coined the formulation of "the function of my God-concepts" in liberation theology, totally in accordance with the general approach of this book. In her approach of the "Sacred Gaia" she tries to establish a wholeness of different "-scapes" as "SocialScape" and "PoeticScape", where she uses Christian traditions in favour of an universal Earth spirituality, which to me often seems to be more interested in general ontological modes of relating to nature's being in general than in modes of transforming human acting in and in regard to nature.

[40] An ambitious survey on all contemporary fields of research about and practice of "religion and nature" is at present in the stage of development in the editing project of an Encyclopedia of Religion and Nature edited by Bron Taylor and Jeffrey Kaplan, forthcoming 2003 at Continuum, London/New York. Cf. e.g. my entry on "Christianity and Nature in Europe".

[41] Rappaport, pp. 27–42.

[42] In the diocese of Lund in the Lutheran Swedish Church an ecotheologically inspired process of renewing liturgy has been developed in the 90's.

[43] For an extensive discussion of aesthetics and its different notions and for an interpretation of the ongoing "processes of aesthetisation" see Welsch, Chapter I, and for its significance for a contextual theology of arts see Bergmann (2002a), Chapter IV.1.4.

[44] The creative manifold of such a reconstruction of Christian theology in the light of the ecological challenge is wonderfully shown by the anthology of Southern and Northern perspectives on ecotheology in Hallman.

Chapter 6

Art and Context

Visual Arts and Theology

There are four reasons for developing the dialogue between the visual arts and theology.[1]

First, apart from the production of texts, the history of Christianity has created a great number of pictures, sculptures and buildings through which artists have interpreted the Christian faith and worldview. Not until the 19th century were art and theology disengaged. Theologians retired to an increasingly secluded sphere and left public translation of reality to natural scientists and artists.[2]

In modern society, art is created autonomously, even if it retains a living metaphysics, unlike the natural sciences which believes it functions with neutral value judgements. So art partly refers to the Christian iconography but is largely influenced by a creative re-interpretation of freely chosen metaphysical parts from non-Christian and esoterical beliefs.

While the theology of icons in the Early Church's tradition and pre-modern Christianity constituted a main agent for theology's construction it has declined during modern times.

Second, visual arts represent an intuitive and rational interpretation of reality, which deserves the designation science. Art studies in western society are given as a part of the academy's activities, even if its epistemological potential is far from being exhausted in an adequate way.

The visual arts express perspectives on the context of culture, environment and society in a way, which makes visible and transcends prevailing patterns of perception. A picture of art can transform the gaze of the beholder and thereby his/her relation to nature. Art elucidates and illuminates problems and processes reflexively.

It further contains a great deal of experimental urge and play, and hereby wins a normative frankness, which works as a constant corrective to threatening cultural rigidity.

The expressions of art, and especially the expressions of pictorial art, visualize life- and worldviews. They shape the system of norms and signs, often with a surprisingly large religious wisdom, knowledge and consciousness.

This second reason for the interaction of contextual theology with pictorial art may be summed up in a formula: "The art pictures make visible the same crucial problems unavoidable in their present cultural context to which the Christian interpretation of life, with its specific qualifications, ought to contribute to finding solutions."[3]

Third, pictorial art offers an alternative of action, which may win great importance for the fellowship of the faithful. In a state of society which sociologists describe as dominated by instrumental goal rationality, the aimless creating of the arts contributes with criticism of this state and assists in a new, widened rationality. The creation of art in itself we may understand as an expression of a practical, aesthetic and critical reason.

In the theology of liberation, the spiral "see-interpret-act" has been developed and in this one concentrates mainly upon the connection between experience and reflection (see-interpret) and between interpretation and acting (interpret-act). On the other hand, one tends to often block out the significant connection between acting and perceiving/experience (act-see). An in-depth dialogue with the competence of art to make possible and visible sensual experiences in a perspective changing way, could lead theology to valuable new discoveries.

We must not, though, idealize art and forget that the power of money,[4] has forced large parts of creativity into the cold or the laws of the shopkeeper's market. Since the days of Baudelaire, art has been transformed into "prostitution". Nonetheless, the financial approach to life has not succeeded in suffocating the creativity, which constantly breaks through in different forms and in new places.

The challenge to contextual theology in the pastoral sphere consists of co-operation with the creators of art without the churches making them into tools for their own aims. The freedom of art is a necessary part of its essence, which it also shares with theology.[5] What the modernists in Vienna at the turn of the century wrote in block letters above the portal of the "Sezession" building is valid for the arts as well as for theology: "To · each · era · its · art · To · each · art · its · freedom!"

A fourth reason lies in the fact that since the breakthrough of modernism in the first world pictorial art in the third and fourth worlds has had a very significant meaning for art's critical perspective on the industrialized form of life.

Art in the third world and among indigenous populations is at present in a very dynamic phase of development within which arises a totally new sign system for communication between artists in places in the different worlds.[6] We ought to ask ourselves, therefore, how this intercultural creating of art relates to the dynamic transcontextual theology.

Art in Context

I will now depart from a contextual perspective on art meaning that we will observe the creation process of a work of art in a similar way to how we understood the creation of a theological interpretation of life.

To what extent one can compare these two processes poses a problem, which we for the present will disregard. Contextual art theory is still young.[7] The artists themselves have, without using the notion "context", long worked in a very high consciousness of cultural and ecological contexts. In a proper sense, the notions "contextual perspective on art", "context-art", and "art in context" are applicable only from the 1990s.

The aim of this last chapter is to point to the potential which is concealed in a future dialogue, partly between the context-conscious art and pastoral theology, and partly between history of art and the academic contextual theology. To offer the reader both pictorial and discursive experiences of this potential we will observe and interpret four pieces of art, three pictures and one building. After each interpretation there will be a short account of the picture's/space's theological significance in accordance with the model scheme from the previous chapter.

The three pictures and the architect-designed church and surrounding space have originated in different historical and cultural connections. The selection criteria are iconographical. All expressions refer to the Christ-event. They are composed either around a picture of Christ or around the shape of the cross. I will not interpret the pictures comparatively but immanently. The limited space of this chapter does not allow any deeper analysis of the artist's identity and the creation of the picture in question. Instead I search the pictures and the building in the light of the question: How does the artist make God visible in an earthly and historical context? During the interpretation I will examine the signification of the expression and distinguish between the interpretation's material, plastic, iconic and verbal levels and meanings.[8]

Primitive, Jewish, Powerless – The Last Supper according to Emil Nolde

The north German artist Emil Nolde painted "Das Abendmahl" in 1909.

In his colourful oil painting, Nolde uses an evidently physical expression. The observer's eye follows Nolde's brushstrokes and discerns clearly how the painter put the colour on the canvas and spread it out. The eye can even determine in which sequence the painter coloured the different surfaces of the picture. Not one surface of the picture is without colour. Some colours are laid in several layers. The handling of the colour expresses heaviness, seriousness and earthiness. The material content of the picture also expresses the artist's consciousness of the observer who meets through Nolde, not only the product, the finished work, but also the creation, the process of coming into being of the painting.

Figure 6.1: Emil Nolde, *Das Abendmahl,* 1909

The picture's plastic formation of signification occurs through the colour and shape expression. The colour intensity is greater in the middle of the picture than on the periphery. The fore- and background have the lowest intensity while Christ's shirt has the strongest luminosity.

Nolde contrasts very dark tints against yellow and other lighter colour tones. The faces and hands of the figures are shaped with little blackness while, on the other hand, the clothes, the table and the space between are shaped with very dark tones. The choice of colours contrasts rather than completes. The colour tones of the basic colours red, yellow and dark blue carry the shape of the bodies, while the colour in the faces and on the hands have a lighter tint in yellow, green and red.

In this way, Nolde achieves a colour tone contrast between the bodies and the faces in the picture's figures. Light and dark shades in the unclad parts of the bodies, dark and heavy shades on the clad parts of the bodies. The light and warmth is totally concentrated to the midst of the picture. Each face has its special shade and tint; the two faces above to the left because of their brown red shade are warmer and less intensive, while the face of Christ because of its yellow green shade is cooler and more intensive.

Nolde also works with the movement of colours in his picture. The redness in the cloak of the right-hand figure in the foreground corresponds with the left-hand figure at the back and they both correspond with the Saviour's mantle. The colour tones of the lips and the clothes are identical. The backs of the two figures in the front form a kind of entrance for the observer into the picture and the lighter play of light around the picture's middle. The blueness of the chalice is of the same kind though more intensive than in the cloaks in the foreground and on the table.

Nolde's picture lacks a clear moulding of the interspace forms, which intensifies the expression created by the coherent and compact colour composition even more. All shapes are in close connection with each other. Not a single body lacks contact with one of the others. Jesus' body touches six of the disciples' bodies.

The spatial composition lacks extension and depth in the fore-, middle- and background. The depths expressed originate in the faces and not in the space. The shapes are recurrently robust and at the same time soft, square with rounded corners. Technically, Nolde alludes in this way to the so-called primitive art and to the art of the medieval church woodcarvings.

The composition of shape is simple. The two square backs in the front and the two sides of the table carry Jesus' square upper body, which is divided into three parts. Apart from this we find the softer, round and oval shapes in the faces and on the hands. Of special interest is the moulding of the elbows and the inter-space ensuing around them which is very typical of Nolde. The elbow of the right-hand figure in the front creates a triangular shape on the back of the dark figure. There appears a slight depth between the left elbow of the figure in front and

Christ's elbow resting on the table as well as between Christ's elbow and body. The robustly triangular nose at the top on the left also awakens interest. Evidently Nolde consciously refers to what in Germany at the turn of the century was perceived as a Jewish face.[9]

How does the iconic significance of the image arise? Nolde was interested in other cultures as well as in scientific physiognomy. In this picture we find a connection to the primitive art's interpretation of the human body which we also recognize in the art of the Swedish artist Bror Hjorth.

The well-known altar triptych of Hjorth is one of the strongest expressions of contextual, theological pictorial art creating in the Scandinavian history of art. The cultural encounter between the modern and the original is clearly visualized. To the left is the engagingly preaching Lars Levi Læstadius and to the right the receptive Sami. In the middle we see the roughly formed, illuminated Christ all in the subarctic environment of Lapland.

Figure 6.2: Bror Hjorth, *Triptych in the Church of Jukkasjärvi* (in northern Sweden), (postal card)

With Nolde, as with Hjorth, we find a clear will to break with the naturalistic and idealistic forms of the Christ image. Nolde's Saviour is flesh, earthly and Jewish. The fellowship between the men stands out as sincere, intensive, even if dark and weighted down. The eyes of Jesus are closed like in strained prayer. The gazes of the disciples, on the other hand, cross the picture looking at each other or at the Lord.

Through the colour tints and the coherent composition of form Nolde expresses fellowship. The human expressions of togetherness and communication are manifest through the homogeneity and originality in the facial colours.

It is further of interest for art history that Nolde in his moulding of the image's composition refers to Rembrandt's painting "Claudius Civilis".[10] While, according to Rembrandt, Claudius' hand lifts the sword to gather the men to an armed struggle for liberty, the north German Jewish Christ handles his power otherwise.

Claudius' eyes gaze out of the picture towards the coming battle, Christ's eyes close in prayer for the future of the disciples. In the Rembrandt picture, the right-hand figure in the foreground offers the chalice to the King, who prefers, however, the sword. In Nolde's picture, the Prince of peace prepares Himself and the chalice to share it with everyone. Nolde himself comments upon his image of Christ:

> *Christ with a holy, transfigured, totally introspective expression and sitting on both sides and before him the circle of his deeply moved disciples...*[11]

A very interesting significance may be gathered from Nolde's use of the blue colour. It appears as light- and space creating in the chalice, as linear in the faces, and as strokes in the tablecloth and in the left, dark cloak. The blue is the only one of Nolde's colours, which is clear and luminous. The blue imbues the picture. The colour blue, in the art of Nolde's time, often represented the spiritual and it is evident how the artist shapes the blue colour's movement through the parts of the picture, so that it emanates from and returns to the middle, to the chalice which seems not to run dry.

Finally, there is the verbal significance that Nolde expresses in the picture's title: The Lord's Supper. In this picture, Nolde began his concentrated work with the image creating Bible rendering. It may be seen as a starting point for his accompanying religious painting.

We should not misunderstand the image as an illustration. Nolde is not narrating the Eucharist of the Gospel. He is creating the image anew. The painter shapes the same course of events as the Gospel. The oft-mentioned naivety of Nolde should not be misunderstood as biblicism in the sense of his having "translated" the information from the Bible text to the canvas. Nolde read the Bible narratives as text and used all his imagination, his reason, his intuition and his considerable technical knowledge, together with a reconstruction of elements of art history from both the so-called primitive and medieval art and Rembrandt.

Within the above schedule, we can without doubt designate Nolde as a contextual artist in accordance with the synthetic model.

He attaches great importance to the Jewish culture in which the Last Supper and the first Eucharist were celebrated in spite of anti-Semitism being well spread in his surroundings already 1909. He also attaches great importance to the physical and practical experience of the disciples' relations with the Son of God, and with the observer's sensuous contact with the course of action, which strongly expresses the fellowship of the believers. Nolde describes a situation with a strongly liberating power not only for the disciples but for believers of all times. With our gaze we can observe the events and go into them. The observer partakes in the fellowship of the repast.

Nolde further attaches great importance to the historical dimension by using the so-called primitive religion's expressive way of description, though he was more interested in the indigenous people's aesthetics than their way of life and situation during his voyage in Oceania. We are able to interpret his work by the help of what we have called the anthropological, the praxis oriented and the correlation model.

It is further of significance that Nolde was deeply religious in a political societal context, which made it all the more difficult to emphasize God's redeeming presence among non-Europeans and Jews. It should be clear, that the painter through his painting has shown a high degree of consciousness of his cultural, theological, and political context. Even if the word "contextual" entered into a union with the word "theology" only sixty-four years after the creation of the painting, I hope that the rendering of "Das Abendmahl" has shown that apart from his artistic mastery Nolde deserves the title "contextually image creating Bible theologian".

Dead and Resurrected in the People's Body – Pietà according to Mirjam-Rose Ungunmerr-Baumann

During the years 1974 and 1975, the Aboriginal artist Mirjam-Rose Ungunmerr-Baumann created a series of fourteen paintings. These depict the fourteen Stations of the Cross on the path of Jesus' suffering, from Pontius Pilate to the Laying in the grave. The pictures embellish the church, built in 1961, in Daly River in northern Australia.

While Nolde's painting of The Last Supper got its motif from the beginning of the Lord's Passion, we will now scrutinize a motif from its end: "The Thirteenth Station: Mary holds Jesus' dead body".

Figure 6.3: Mirjam-Rose Ungunmerr-Baumann, *Thirteenth Station: Mary holds Jesus' dead body*, 1984

Ungunmerr-Baumann attains the plastic forming of signification through a very sparing choice of colours and austere and simple play of forms. The colours black, white and orange create a harmonic tint of colours. The tint is dark. The bodies and the cross are shaped in black and white, the landscape background in darker and lighter orange. The observer clearly sees in which sequence the artist has applied the colours: first the background's orange tints on the whole picture surface, then the black surfaces of the body and the cross, and lastly the white colour.

Ungunmerr-Baumann thereby follows the traditional technique of the Aborigine's picture making, where one often group-wise colours the surfaces and then, in a given order, introduces a large amount of coded signs in the pictorial space. Through the technique of over-painting, the dark body surfaces as well become faintly differentiated in the power of luminescence.

The black coloured shapes in the picture are without exception soft and round. Only the angle between the long beam and the transverse beam of the cross is sharp. On the other hand, the white coloured shapes show a richer diversity. Points, long stretched bent ellipses, line triangles, parallels and squares are found in different scales in what to the

Westerner seems an unknown pattern. In the lower part of the painting there are also black dots on the surface that are made translucent by the background.

The painting's composition consists of a diagonal which ends in the upper right-hand corner and meets the angle of the Cross. The two bodies make up a total continuous unity of form. Iconographically we could interpret this unity as a sitting or lying body with two heads.

The picture lacks the shaping of volume, which the Western observer readily seeks and who since the Renaissance has been fostered in the pictorial space of central perspective. The white lines and dots emphasize the significance of the surface. Nonetheless, an effect of depth occurs, for example, in the left of the image where Mary's arm embraces the lap of her son. Between her knees and his back, as well, occurs a certain depth.

The iconographic significance demands really a longer investigation of the Australian aboriginal people's worldview, religion and art. The wisdom of this culture, which constitutes the current human race's oldest, is difficult to understand because of its great difference to the Western culture, so I can only express a few preliminary observations.

Ungunmerr-Baumann is herself a confessing catholic Christian and she manages a school of art for Aboriginal Christians. The picture was created as the result of a commission to embellish a church, and its intention is to let the traditional Aboriginal understanding of reality interpret the passion of which the Gospel tells.

Ungunmerr-Baumann locates this course of events to Australia. She describes Mary and Jesus as persons among the aboriginal population of the desert.

The painting cannot be reduced to an inculturation of the missionary's God to the older culture. The Christ of Ungunmerr-Baumann is an Aboriginal and Mary is an Aboriginal woman in whose body the Son is resurrected. The artist raises the cross in the desert landscape of northern Australia.

Four main signs carry the iconic signification of the picture: the landscape, the cross, Mary and Christ. One may also describe the fundamental signification in accordance with the pattern of order for the colouring of the picture: orange, black and white.

In that case, orange denotes the sandy soil and the surrounding landscape, which embraces life. Black denotes the embodidness, the material of the wood, and the flesh of the body. White denotes the signs, which, with the help of a complicated code system that only initiated Aboriginal artists know of, express the spiritual significance

of the painting. To understand the significance of the white layer, we
enlist the help of Ungunmerr-Baumann herself:

> *An Aboriginal mother can only comfort a grown-up son in sorrow*
> *by touching him with her hand, but once he has died, she can*
> *take his body into her arms for the last time. Mary's body and*
> *her son's merge into one. The tear in Mary's head and on her*
> *hand symbolize her sorrow, as in the Fourth Station, but this time*
> *straight lines radiate out from the tear as a sign of her new life*
> *from her dead son. Christ dead in her arms is alive in her person.*
> *She carries him anew and will mother him again, as the first*
> *Christian and as Mother of the Church. The resurrection, just*
> *like the incarnation itself, is already taking place in Mary through*
> *faith before it takes place actually in Christ.*
>
> *Mary's body and your body are one, Jesus. Your life lives on in*
> *her body. She carries on your life in herself.*[12]

Even if the Gospels do not record if Mary is active at the care-taking
of the dead body, the conception of the touch between the mother and
the son's dead body has inspired artists during time and led to a special
motif tradition: the pietà. The Gospels do not tell if Mary, mother
of Jesus, was present when Joseph from Arimataia took the body and
shrouded it, but records that "the other Mary" and Mary from Magdala
"were there" (Matthew 27:61) and that they "saw where he was put"
(Mark 15:47).

The painting of Ungunmerr-Baumann is, accordingly, part of a very
old Christian iconographic tradition. In relation to the European pietà
pictures, it is distinguished through the lack of individual, personal
features. Jesus and Mary are people, not individuals whose personal
identity has been carved out of an entire community. In accordance
with the tradition of her people, Ungunmerr-Baumann depicts the human bodies as parts of humanity's common body. The identity of the
individual arises through being a part of the people fellowship.

Seen from this Aboriginal understanding of society, the picture expresses the message of the Gospel, so that the body of mother and son
become one through the care taking of one by the other. The resurrection like the incarnation occurs in the believing Mary. The incarnation
and the bodily resurrection in the artist's conception of the world consist of an ontological course of events.

The border between outer and inner, bodily and spiritually, is not
expressed in the way that the Westerner expects. The signs on the
body surfaces are both physical and spiritual. The oval shape in and
on Mary's head refers to the physical tear, which in its turn refers to

Mary's feeling of sorrow. The parted oval shape of Jesus' lower body refers to the physical stomach, which in its turn refers to the person's spiritual centre.

Observing all the pictures in the series, one discovers how the stomach's shape corresponds with Jesus' condition in relation to the specific station on the road of suffering. In this picture the stomach appears small and resting.

In the interpretation of Ungunmerr-Baumann, that Jesus is "living in her person" we should not understand one-side spiritually. The worldview of the Aboriginals is characterized by spiritual life that is ongoing in a dynamic time-continuum.[13] The Aboriginals do not know of any separation between the bodily and spiritual sphere. The distinction between bodily and spiritual may be paraphrased, so that the body is the bearer of the spiritual. The landscape, animal- and plant life and the people are materialized parts of a common spiritual reality. Without this ongoing spiritual history there is no life. Life begins since the ancestors created the landscape and the signs interact with the living in a way that only individuals initiated into dream time can understand.[14]

In comparison with the late antique metaphysics within which the Christian faith got its shape of dogma, these Aboriginal metaphysics, which rather might be described as pneuma physics (spirit nature), offer an interesting philosophical condition for translating the course of incarnation and resurrection. The Mary of this image stands for the human being, both woman and man, and the spiritual landscape for the creation through which body and soul Christ manifestly arises, physically and visually, within and without.

In conclusion I will make a few remarks on the depiction of landscapes in Ungunmerr-Baumann's pictures. She consistently uses an orange background in two shades, which through the horizontal lines connects with the tradition and technique of Western landscape rendering.

We may understand the lines as horizons and contours of the soil, the mountains or the clouds. The colouring can be related to the dry North Australian climate drenched in sand and sun. In spite of Ungunmerr-Baumann applying a traditional form for the plastic and iconic expression in the description of the figures and the cross, she chooses background with a conventional perspective and for the West a typical expression. Why?

Is the intention here as well to fuse together Aboriginal and Western ways of perceiving pictures? Or is the shaping of the background a concession to the gaze of the immigrant and the colonizer?

Following a comparison of the two pictures the answer becomes slightly more complicated. Ungunmerr-Baumann consistently shapes the surrounding landscapes in correspondence to the respective iconic expression. When Jesus falls, the horizon is high and the light seems to stream out of the earth. When Jesus is nailed to the cross, the border is drawn between heaven and earth in the shape of a wide, dark stream (perhaps the stream by which the church lies) right through the intersection point between the crossbars and Jesus' head.

In spite of the Western technique of description, Ungunmerr-Baumann follows a traditional Aboriginal and Biblical way of thinking: the landscape shares the suffering of Christ. The means of expression for this message are few. Only the small nuances in the tint and the lines carry the iconic expression.

Another way of expressing the same content, the landscape's participation in the Crucifixion refers to the traditional Aboriginal landscape rendering. Neville Japangardi Poulson describes the ground surface from a bird's eye view. On the "myth map" of topographical formations, the artist inserts the signs, which denote the spiritual and, therefore, the actual physical history of the landscape. The snake's shape refers to the Aborigine myth of Creation. The ring formations denote places of holy events and in the left lower part of the image we find the signs of the Crucifixion. In this image as well, Jesus' road of suffering is expressed if only more consequently topologically. The signs that the artist has distributed across the surface denote different meaning for stations and contents on Jesus' way to and from the cross.

Figure 6.4: Neville Japangardi Poulson, *Passion*, 1988

The pictures of Ungunmerr-Baumann and Japangardi Poulson express a contextual theology in the medium of image creation. Ungunmerr-Baumann's pietà does not merely constitute an illustration of the Bible text but makes claim to being an interpretation of the ongoing mystery of revelation, incarnation and resurrection. The picture cannot be interpreted in a conventional perspective of inculturation either, as Christianity's static message does not become "implanted" into the Aboriginal worldview.

Ungunmerr-Baumann's picture supplies something qualitatively new to the interpretation of Jesus and Mary's suffering when she lets the Aboriginal religion illuminate the mystery of the bodily union of the believer and the dead person. We may even ask if this Australian pneuma-physics might carry a considerably larger potential for making justice to the worldview of the Gospels than the Western meta-physics which often tended to reduce the Biblical expressions for the resurrection of the flesh.

In accordance with our diagram of models, we can characterize Ungunmerr-Baumann's picture as an expression of an anthropological and correlational contextual theology. The picture expresses a high degree of cultural consciousness of the Aboriginal and Western worldview on the Christ-event and the revelation. It aims intensively at a credible synthesis between the Aboriginal culture and the Biblical belief in regard to God and the world. It would be worth an examination of to what degree this picture also is able to illuminate the traditional Aboriginal belief in spirit and landscape.

Interestingly enough, Emil Nolde also devoted himself to the same motif as Ungunmerr-Baumann, namely the care taking of the dead body of Christ. In Nolde's picture "Grablegung" from 1915, we see Mary concealed behind Jesus' head.[15] Nolde's Mary as well embraces the body. Nolde shapes the bodily union between the two figures as expressively and intensively as Ungunmerr-Baumann. The two images express similar iconic interpretations of the bodily union between the living mother and the dead son.

The difference between the two images is evident. The Aboriginal rendering expresses resurrection through the dead body. The North German rendering lets Jesus' body be dead and all life is localized with those who take care of Him. The resurrection in North Germany takes place through Mary and the disciples, while in Australia it takes place in a spiritual transformation between the bodies. Jesus by Nolde is dead and Mary tries to press him back into her womb. Ungunmerr-Baumann depicts Jesus as physically dead (the expression of the stomach) and

Figure 6.5: Mirjam-Rose Ungunmerr-Baumann, *Thirteenth Station: Mary holds Jesus' dead body*, 1984

simultaneously resurrected in and through Mary.

Landscape, Body and Culture – Sami Crucifixion according to Unni Myrseth

Like the Australian Aboriginals, the Sami people see the landscape as a carrier of spiritual meaning. In 1992 the Sami artist Unni Myrseth paints "Kulturlandskap", (Cultural Landscape).

The cultural landscape has a complicated composition of form. One diagonal divides the image into three parts. Below the diagonal we find several complex angular and multi-sided shapes. Above it we meet only brush strokes, a black dot, soft narrow and long small shapes which arise between the surface paint and the dark colour.

The rock and ground formations express a very differentiated spatiality which is reinforced by the contrast effects between the yellow and green tints and the black covering colour. The foreground and the lower part of the picture are composed of five different elements of form.

The variations of form bring about different expressions of nearness and distance. The shaping of the interspace forms carry the expression of the image leading and beguiling the observer's orientation in the landscape. Myrseth slowly builds up the long beam from out of the play of the rock forms. The transverse beam arches a long narrow

Figure 6.6: Emil Nolde, *Grablegung*, 1915

triangle with its point in the upper spherical part of the picture. The body of Christ is one with the cross. Only the forms of the interspace and the two yellow tints make it possible for the observer to interpret the form as a body. The left transverse beam becomes one with the arm of Christ.

The scale of colours is yellow and green tints and black in different combinations in all parts of the picture. The strongest luminescence is in the body's yellows and the weakest we find in the upper left part of the painting. On the ground the yellow dominates over the green and the green predominates in the sky. The colour contrasts are graphic rather than picturesque. Myrseth colours the sky, the body and the ground in the same scale while the black colour is used for the shaping of space and depth.

The artist's brushstrokes create several different expressions. The wide, linear brushstrokes contrast with the covering colour of the small yellow surfaces and the transparent colouring in the fore and middle ground.

Which iconic content do these plastic expressions create? Looking at the tradition of European landscape painting the question turns out to be problematic. It is indubitably so, that landscape pictures convey a content and message which we may interpret as representations of different moments of life-view. Even if Myrseth refers to this tradition

Figure 6.7: Unni Myrseth, *Kulturlandskap*, 1993

of landscape painting, a perspective of interpretation of this kind seems misleading for the elucidation of her pictorial production. The painting's title "Cultural Landscape" gives us a hint of this. That which a citizen in a large town regards as wilderness is here described as cultural landscape. Where is the culture visible? Is it in the Crucifixion?

Iconically the observer recognizes the formal elements of the landscape: the ground, stones, mountains, clouds and sky. The white colour, which runs diagonally through the picture may by translated as a snow-clad mountainside. On the green yellow ground surface we recognize low growing bushes. In this way, the ground surfaces change between snow covered ground and ground which is nourishing for the reindeer.

For the reindeer herding Sami, the knowledge of the soil, snow and vegetation is a necessary prerequisite to the survival of the reindeer and the own group. In Myrseth's picture, the cultural element rests with this point of view in the gaze of the observer at the physical character of the landscape, which on its part, offers itself to cultivation as grazing ground.

The play of forms in and between the white and green yellow surfaces stands out as stone, rock, mountains and mountain massifs. In the picture's different spatial pictorial worlds, Myrseth creates a distance between the near and distant mountain area. This is overwhelming in a way only manifest in the mountain and fjord world of northern Norway. The richness in the spatial dimension between the foot of the Golgatha hill and the white mountain-slope in the distance seem to overpower an observer used to the open cultivated landscape of southern Sweden. The plastic manifestation of the figure of the cross conveys a physically marked feeling of participation. The figure both rises out of the landscape and in a mysterious way goes back into its depth.

Theologically, I would interpret the culture landscape of Myrseth in the light of the biblical conceptions of the cosmic and earthly Christ. The Christ figure is totally shaped by the help of landscape elements. The Crucified is landscape. The landscape is nailed to his cross.

The cosmos and the historical-earthly human God melt together, as the Saviour is the Creator. The plastic manifestation of the colour motion creates a lightness, which through the snow, wind and cloud spheres contrast against the weight of the rocks. The figure of Christ is drawn into this motion in spite of being anchored to the ground.

We may perhaps interpret the symbol of the wind and the colour motion as a sign of the Spirit who, according to the Scriptures, blows where she wishes and, among others, may awake Jesus from the dead.

To me personally, the body stance of Christ reminds me of the swallow, which with quick and sure wing-strokes bathes in the air stream. It is interesting, that the Sami religion knows of the "Vearalden Olmai", "The Man of the World", divinity of heaven and upholder of the world, and whose name refers to the fertility of the soil.[16] The Christian missionaries readily referred to this Sami interpretation of God when preaching about the relation between the Father and the Son in the Christian Trinity. Maybe the Man of the World died with the Crucified and is resurrected in the Sami cultural landscape?

The picture makes an example of a contextually pictoral creating theology. The landscape, the Creation, and Christ the human God correspond with each other. Myrseth depicts Christ as transparent and plastic in a dynamic and dramatic landscape space. The landscape shines through and on his body. It gets meaning and content through the cross of the Saviour. The landscape partakes in the Crucifixion. Will it partake in the Resurrection as well?

The creation of the picture is ongoing in accordance with the anthropological model as Myrseth uses her knowledge of the Sami culture's understanding of the landscape and practical relation to it. Snow, ground vegetation, wind, clouds and distance, are signs of specific importance in the Sami culture. The Gospel is expressed in this picture wholly on the condition of the physical landscape in Sami country and through Sami eyes. The Crucifixion of the Creator and of Creation takes place in Sápmi, the land of the Sami.

There is a correlation intention missing in Myrseth's picture, as we do not find any signs referring to pre-Christian or the new spiritual Sami religion. One could possibly interpret some of the crevices according to the conception of holy sites expressed aesthetically by the way of specific forms. This interpretation though, to such a high degree presupposes initiated knowledge of the topographical aesthetics of the Sami religion, that I will exclude it here.

The picture of Unni Myrseth tends towards what we above called the human ecological model. The human being, the Creator and the Creation are the three structural theological elements constituting the painting. The picture lends the space a very expressive spiritual signification. Myrseth hereby gives the preference to Creation within which living space is played out the historical drama of men, women and nature's painful liberation.

A Spiritual Landscape of the Cross – "Church on the Water" by Tadao Ando

The spiritual signification of space becomes especially clear in "Church on the Water", designed by Tadao Ando and erected in 1985-1988.

Figure 6.8: Tadao Ando, *Church on the Water*, 1995

The church is situated in the Hokkaido Mountain's high range in

Japan. In summer the building is imbedded in lush greenery. The winter of this cold region clothes it in masses of snow.

The church does not belong to any parish. It is above all used for marriage ceremonies celebrated by the priests of the region and arranged by the nearby retreat centre of Furano.[17] The surrounding environment constitutes the parish of the church. According to Asian tradition, nature elements as well belong to the believers.

The compound consists of several overlapping squares which have been built around the borders of an artificial pond. The pond was constructed through drawing off water from a nearby stream. A free-standing wall in the shape of an L encloses the rear of the church and one side of the pond.

As evident from the drawings the building is composed of three levels. The church hall and the pond surface constitute the lowest level. The entrance hall lies on a hillock on an upper level and above this lies a hall of light with glass walls open to all points of the compass. The church entrance is in the back. The visitor is met by a secretive murmuring of water without being able to pin point its source. By moving in a half circle downwards around the inner free standing wall one reaches the view point towards the wide water surface of the pond.

At the entrance to the church, you turn to the left and ascend a small staircase into the glassed-in vestibule. The glass windows are held up by a cross-shaped girder construction forming a "box of light".

In the church hall, only the benches meet the visitor. The glass windows do duty as the altar and in this the cross rises out of the water which is surrounded by a landscape in five parts consisting of the pond, the edge of the pond, the formation of trees, the mountain slope and the sky. The framework of the stone wall on the left-hand side opens up the horizon towards the mountain gives depth and perspective to the natural space and ties it to the position of the viewer in the space. The outer surface of the pond and the inner surface of the floor melt together as one scene.

The compound is structured throughout by the idiom of the square and the cross. In the upper cube of glass and on the roof the cross creates four smaller squares within the square. The same play of forms returns in the wall and in the free standing sculpture in the middle of the glass room.

In this way, the observer may understand the cross in the pond as something, which creates atmosphere around itself. Specific spaces appear around the cross girders in a play between the observer, the water and the landscape. What is distant in the background comes closer and the foreground melts together with the background. The space created by the cross around itself functions as a condensation and optical middle point for the whole surroundings. The cross, though, is not placed in the middle of the pond but in its left part near the church hall. Thus the perspective remains entirely open and follows the mountain ridge rising out of the horizon.

Tadao Ando belongs to the most distinguished of the now living architects. His designed sites are considered the finest creations of the 1980s anywhere in the world.[18] The reason to consider his churches and their surroundings in our context is Ando's conscious creation of a Christian space in correlation with the local physical environment and the spiritual space that the Japanese tradition offers. With the same openness that the Church on the Water shows its surroundings we may interpret his building in relation to the religious surrounding world.

Through the shallow barrage of the water surface the architect conjures up the traditional Japanese concept of "oku". The notion oku means the inner, the inward. This inner may lie in the distance and it may lie near. Oku is a kind of invisible middle point. Within the limits of a sea one may imagine that there is oku. Even within the house being cared for by the woman one may imagine oku. Ando's church conjures up oku through the cross in the shallow water. This brings us closer to what lies distantly and it unites the interior of the building with its exterior.

Another traditional connection lies in the notion of the sacred place or the holy shrine, "tokonoma". This place may refer to a wall in a family dwelling or a special part of it where, according to Buddhism or the Shinto religion, one places a holy object for worship. In the Buddhist tradition the word denotes both the temple and the mountain. To a believing Buddhist, the signification holy place and mountain are, therefore, inseparable notions. Ando's Church on the Water constitutes such a "tokonoma". It creates a religious centre for which the mountain landscape not only forms the background. On the contrary, the landscape, the mountain and the Church on the Water constitute a coherent regional focal point in a religious natural universe. The ascent of the mountain range gains an important meaning in this universe.

In the Shinto tradition the mountain as well as the temple melt together. There one may even talk about an ontological meaning according to which the mountain itself is the sacred place. This point of view is also expressed very strongly in the experience of the Church on the Water. The mountain is the temple, the Creator is present in the inner and the outer space, and the landscape is the temple. The Shinto portal, "Torii", often stands in a shallow pond and expresses the entrance to this sacred room. A Japanese visitor immediately understands the cross in Ando's spiritual landscape as being in direct connection with the holy gate, "Torii".

A third interpretation of the Church on the Water originates from the tradition of mandala, which is a symbolic expression of the religious universe. Like the symbol in the Western perspective, mandala does not simply refer to the religious sphere, which surpasses the natural sphere. The mandala manifests this reality and at the same times symbolizes it. In other words, the spiritual arises simultaneously as one refers to it through some expression.

Ando's structure links up with the Zen Buddhism, which carries mandala out into nature. Zen Buddhism attaches to the natural space a leading significance of spiritual reality. The shaping of the landscape wins in this tradition an all-pervading spiritual import. When the human believer shapes his/her place and their space of the surroundings he/she at the same time manifests a spiritual presence. The spatial configuration becomes a holy act, a sacrament. If we interpret the Church on the Water as such a mandala, it appears at the same time as a referring symbol to the biblical Crucifixion and to the redeeming history of the salvation. It appears as an ongoing course of events in which the Crucifixion and the Resurrection quite tangibly are played out in the physical and spiritual landscape scene.

A fourth interpretation of Ando's spiritual landscape originates from the importance of light. The box of light in the upper elevation of the construction serves both as a light inlet for the inner room and as an outlook to experience the play of light in the surroundings. The shadows of the cross fall in lively and changing patterns on the surfaces inside the room. The light of the church hall is entirely fetched from the surrounding's reflections of the lights in the sky. The pond's water surface throws the light back and up towards heaven.

The mystery of light here appears in as conscious a configuration as in the medieval cathedrals in Europe. In all his projects, Ando very consciously works with the light and its power to change the expression and experience of the building through the passage of time.[19] We find the same competence as in an important part of Gothic architecture.

With this, Ando manages something of a feat, making it possible for an Asian visitor to the church to understand him/herself in the place by the help of a classic Buddhist, a Zen Buddhist, a Shinto and/or a Christian worldview. Furthermore, he ably relates to the postmodern architecture and its discourse on the shaping of meaning. Ando differs from his colleagues, though, who represent a relativistic postmodernism, and he chooses instead to consciously integrate traditions in their cultural context without deconstructing them. If anything, the traditions win deepening and renewal through Ando's spiritual landscape. Through his building, the Western understanding of Christianity with its one-eyed understanding of the meaning of the symbol is challenged. The symbol in church architecture is never only referring but always both referring and manifesting simultaneously. Architecture is always function and vision; it points beyond itself by expressing itself in a larger space.[20] In this way, we can understand church architecture as a metaphor for the incarnation and, at the same time, as a manifestation of incarnation itself. With this we may be helped by the late antique theological thought of the Holy Spirit's inhabitation, the Spirit which takes its dwelling.[21]

In Ando's programmatic shaping of the school of thought which architectural historians denote as "critical regionalism",[22] we meet yet another point of reference to contextual theology's emphasizing the significance of local connections.

Critical regionalism at the same time is a criticism of the utopia and optimization ideal of modernity and a continuity of the modern confidence in the liberation of humankind. In this school one does not emphasize the autonomy of the building but it assumes a specific place in which a new human building will arise. Regionalism is aware of the tectonic configuration, but it understands this above all as a creation in relation to the flow of light according to the specific conditions of the place. The tactile is seen as equally important as the visual. Critical regionalism wants to construe the building not as a detached local entity but sees it in a more uniform universal context. In other words, it seeks a solution to the problem discussed above, i.e. the universalizing of local entities. The school of critical regionalism, within which Ando designed a masterpiece also of the Japanese art of building, we may regard as a historical parallel to the growth of contextualism in the theological sphere.

It ought to be clearly apparent, that we may count Ando, with his formation of the Church on the Water and its underlying thoughts, among artists creating in a contextual theological manner. The Church on the Water is distinguished by a high consciousness of religious culture, of interreligious fellowship of interpretation and of the Christian iconography's language limits. It also consciously relates to a Zen Buddhist and a late-modern ecological understanding of nature's and the landscape's spiritual meaning. The landscape though does not appear as a romantic mirror surface, but as a space to which man is challenged to express him/herself creatively. Ando himself expresses it thus:

> My goal has not been to commune with nature as it is but rather
> to change the meaning of nature through architecture. I believe
> that when that happens man will discover a new relationship with
> nature.[23]

The designing of the natural space is a practical and spiritual task. The designing itself manifests the sacredness. The designing, the construction and the use of the Church on the Water is an expression of the ongoing incarnation of God, which in this book has been designated as the main characteristics of contextual theology. In Ando's spiritual landscape of the cross, we meet a God in function, a God who together with men and women transfigures the sacred places of Creation, tokonoma, in relation to its inner, oku. In this landscape a new relation arises between Creation, men/women and Creator.

Summary

What could the interpretation of these three paintings and the church building teach contextual theology?

Arguments against my mode of procedure could be raised with assertions that here we do not at all find worked-up interpretations of Christianity but only fragments of Christian and other interpretations of life.

After all, Myrseth merely presents a picture of a cross in a landscape, Ungunmerr-Baumann only a body in an Australian desert, and Nolde gives his personal image of the word from the Bible. Ando is only experimenting with abstract idioms.

The objection may be justified if one only looks at aesthetic expressions as expressions of personal motives and thoughts. An art picture though, expresses content in a much more manifold way compared to the text. It is distinguished through its concurrence of material, plastic, and iconic expressions. The ambiguity, which is not arbitrary but created, offers a medium of expression, which in the restricted space of the picture canvas opens for insights enriching theology qualitatively. In the medium of architecture it is also in addition the possibility of forming a three-dimensional space of experience and action.

The aim with these interpretations of pictures and built spaces has been to mediate an experience of the richness, which an artistic expression offers contextual theology. I have further tried to argue that the pictures and the building themselves compose theological expressions.

The three images of Christ and the theology of the sacral landscape space are not only expressed through the use of Christian symbols and references. They are expressed above all through the way of shaping. Pictorially, graphically and expressively Nolde, Ungunmerr-Baumann and Myrseth stand out as contextual theologians. Ando, with his designed building in the landscape space, stands out as a contextual theologian of religion.

The four interpretations contextualize a rendering of the Gospel in a specific ecological, social and cultural situation. Exactly because of this contextual unicity, the four images of God possess a mysterious endurance in space and time. We can, therefore, interpret the creating of picture and space in analogy to the theologians who by means of the text reflect upon God in function.

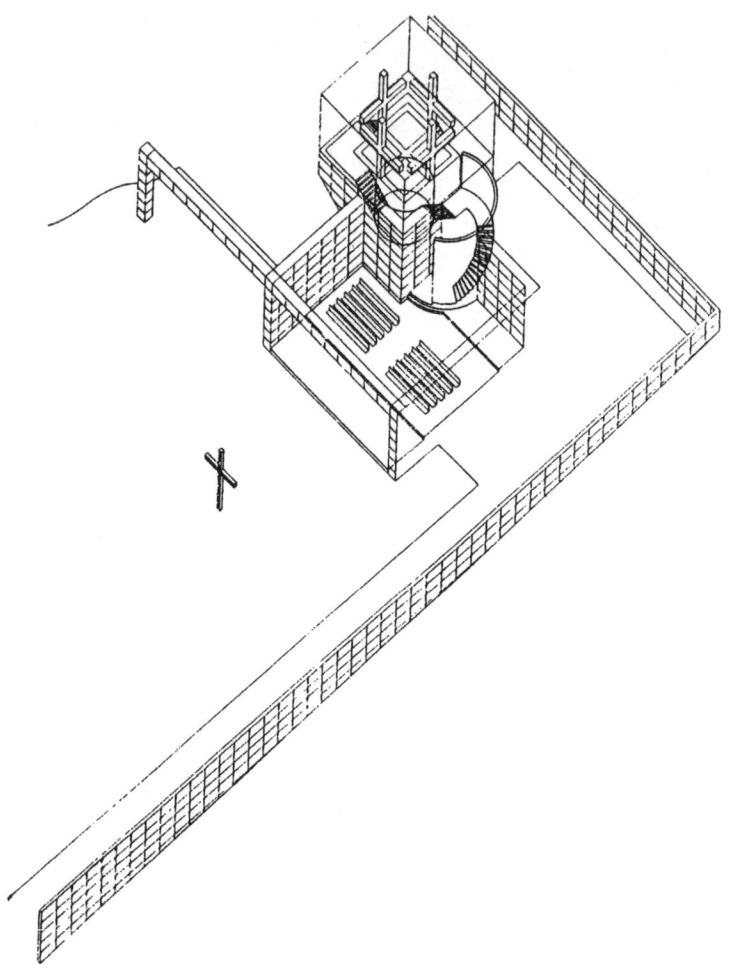

Figure 6.9: Tadao Ando, *Church on the Water*, bird's-eye axonometric

Figure 6.10: Tadao Ando, *Church on the Water*

Notes

[1] The issues and reflections on the encounter of the visual arts and theology in this chapter are developed in my forthcoming monograph: *I begynnelsen är bilden: en befriande bild-konst-kultur-teologi*, Stockholm: Proprius 2002, (*In The Beginning Is The Image: A Liberating Theology of Visual Arts In Culture*).

[2] An extensive "history of the image" is offered by Belting who in spite of his excellent art historic competence is bound to a reductionist and polemical understanding of theology in and around the images.

[3] Bergmann (1994b), p. 60.

[4] In his extensive cultural-sociological study of the autonomy of money and the financial system, Georg Simmel wrote already in 1900, p. 483, on "money's lack of character" (die Charakterlosigkeit des Geldes) and the objectification of human beings which is caused by that. "Philosophie des Geldes", Berlin 7. edition 1977 (1900). The connection between arts and the pursuit of financial profits in capitalist business-making has been discussed by Theodor W. Adorno, pp. 467–468, in: "Ästhetische Theorie", Frankfurt am Main 13. edition 1995 (1970). The historical development of monetarism from merchantilism to our present globalized world capitalism and its autonomous dynamics of money-accumulation has been shown by Duchrow (1994), pp. 32–39.

[5] Cf. Schleiermacher in: Bergmann (1994b), p. 85.

[6] Cf. Ströter Bender, pp. 8–15, and the important, London-edited, journal *Third Text*.

[7] Cf. Wolfgang Kemp's research seminary in Germany "Kunst im Kontext" and the anthology edited by Weibel (1994): "Kontext Kunst". The well-known publishing house Dumont started 1995 the edition of its ambitious series *art in context*, published in German and English.

[8] According to Sjölin, pp. 62–67.

[9] Nolde was on the one hand criticized for his pictorial experimenting with a "cultural relativism", and on the other hand he stayed faithful, e.g. in the painting "The Life of Christ" (1912) to his seeking for "absolute certainty" regarding the Christian and the European. On the tension between intellectual open mindedness and Eurocentric universalism in

Nolde's work see Lloyd, pp. 212–234.

[10]Cf. Købke Sutton.

[11]Quoted after Købke Sutton, p. 34.

[12]Ungunmerr-Baumann, p. 28.

[13]Cf. Curuana, p. 10. A survey on the spirituality of the Aboriginal people in relationship to the identity of the Australian nation is offered by the catholic archeologian Eugene Stockton. On the differences between the Western and Aboriginal worldviews see Stockton, pp. 37–49.

[14]Cf. Curuana, pp. 10–14, and Stockton, pp. 81–87.

[15]Cf. my interpretation of this painting in Bergmann (1994b), pp. 82–84.

[16]Cf. Bäckman, pp. 76–77.

[17]According to information given by Masao Takenaka (the nestor of visual Christian Arts and Theology in Asia, and editor of the journal *Image: Christian Arts in Asia*).

[18]Frampton, p. 341.

[19]Cf. Frampton, p. 325.

[20]Cf. Bergmann (1996b).

[21]On Ando's interreligious relevance especially and on the relationship between spirituality, Christian pneumatology and architecture generally see my essay "Space and Spirit: Towards a Theology of Inhabitation" forthcoming in the anthology including contributions to the symposium "Architecture, Aesth/Ethics and Religion", Trondheim, May 2001. For a rich historical investigation in the same field see Sheldrake.

[22]Cf. Frampton, p. 327.

[23]Quoted after Frampton, p. 342.

Bibliography

Altner, G. (1991), *Naturvergessenheit. Grundlagen einer umfassenden Bioethik*, Darmstadt.

Arens, E. (1991), 'Kommunikative Rationalität und Religion. Die Theorie des kommunikativen Handelns als Herausforderung politischer Theologie', in Arens, E., John, O. and Rottländer, P. (eds), *Erinnerung, Befreiung, Solidarität. Benjamin, Marcuse, Habermas und die politische Theologie*, Düsseldorf, pp.145-200.

Århem, P. (1995), 'Antropologins mening. En introduktion', in Århem, P. (ed), *Den antropologiska erfarenheten*, Stockholm, pp.9-37.

Ateek, N. S., Ellis, M. H. and Radford Ruether, R. (eds) (1992), *Faith and the Intifada. Palestinian Christian Voices*, Maryknoll.

Bäckman, L. (1991), 'Vearalden Olmai – Världens Man – Frey eller Kristus?' in Bäckman, L., Drobin, U. and Berglie, P.-A. (eds), *Studier i religionshistoria tillägnade Åke Hultkrantz*, Löberöd, pp.71-96.

Bayer, O. (1990), *Schöpfung als Anrede. Zu einer Hermeneutik der Schöpfung*, 2. ed. Tübingen.

Beck, U. (1986), *Risikogesellschaft. Auf dem Weg in eine andere Moderne*, Frankfurt am Main.

Beck, U. (1988), *Gegengifte. Die organisierte Unverantwortlichkeit*, Frankfurt am Main.

Beck, U. (1993), *Die Erfindung des Politischen. Zu einer Theorie reflexiver Modernisierung*, Frankfurt am Main.

Belting, H. (1991), *Bild und Kult. Eine Geschichte des Bildes vor dem Zeitalter der Kunst*, 2. ed. München (1990), (*Likeness and Presence. A History of the Image before the Era of Art*, Chicago 1994).

Benjamin W. (1991), 'Über den Begriff der Geschichte', in *Gesammelte Schriften. Abhandlungen, Band I, 2*, Frankfurt am Main, pp.691-704.

Berger, P. L. and Luckmann, T. (1977), *Die gesellschaftliche Konstruktion der Wirklichkeit. Eine Theorie der Wissenssoziologie*, 5. ed. Frankfurt am Main, (*The Social Construction of Reality*, New York 1966).

Bergmann, S. (1993), 'Gregory of Nazianzen's Theological Interpretation of the Philosophy of Nature in the Doctrine of the Four Elements', in Livingstone, E. A. (ed), *Studia Patristica Vol. XXVII*, Leuven, pp.3-8.

Bergmann, S. (1994a), 'Diskursiv bioetik – för offrens skull', in Svedin, U. and Thunberg, A.-M. (eds), *Miljöetik – för ett samhälle på människans och naturens villkor*, (Forskningsrådsnämnden Rapport 94:2), Stockholm, pp.68-89.

Bergmann, S. (1994b), '"Landskapet har gått under i dammet" – Den moderna bildkonstens naturbild utmanar kulturteologin', in Bergmann and Bråkenhielm (eds) (1994), pp.57-90.

Bergmann, S. (1995a), *Geist, der Natur befreit. Die trinitarische Kosmologie Gregors von Nazianz im Horizont einer ökologischen Theologie der Befreiung*, Mainz, (in Russian Arkhangelsk 1999, in English (*Creation Set Free*) forthcoming Grand Rapids, Mich. 2003/4).

Bergmann, S. (1995b), 'Natursyn och gudsbild. Om teologins betydelse för miljövetenskapen', in *Tvärsnitt*, vol. 17, no. 4/1995, pp.40-51, ('Naturauffassung und Gottesbild', in Bergmann (1997), pp.178-189).

Bergmann, S. (1996a), 'History of mission – history of liberation?' in Lande, Aa. and Ustorf, W. (eds), *Mission in a Pluralist World*, (Studies in the Intercultural History of Christianity 97), Frankfurt am Main, pp.81-104.

Bergmann, S. (1996b), 'Kulturmiljöetik – för de kommande generationernas skull', in *Nordisk arkitekturforskning*, 3/1997, pp.10-34, ('Ethik der Kulturumwelt', in Bergmann (1997), pp.230-272).

Bergmann, S. (1997), *Geist, der lebendig macht – Lavierungen zur ökologischen Theologie der Befreiung*, Frankfurt am Main.

Bergmann, S. (1998), 'Jord, kultur och Ande – komposten i humanekologisk och teologisk belysning', in Bergmann and Bråkenhielm (eds) (1998), pp.224-250, ('Erde, Kultur und Heiliger Geist. Praktische Theologie des Kompostierens', in Bergmann (1997), pp.296-328).

Bergmann, S. (2001), '"Ich kenne ihre Leiden. Darum bin ich herniedergestiegen ..." – Das neue Paradigma der kontextuellen Theologie', in *Studia Theologica. Scandinavian Journal of Theology*, vol. 55, 1/2001, pp.4-22.

Bergmann, S. (ed) (2001), *"Man får inte tvinga någon" – autonomi och relationalitet i nordisk teologisk tolkning*, Nora.

Bergmann, S. (2002b), 'Transculturality and Tradition – Renewing the Continuous in Late Modernity', forthcoming in Arinin, E. et al. (eds), *2000 Years of Christian Culture and Ethnoses of the Barents Region*, Arkhangelsk, Russia.

Bergmann, S. (2003), *I begynnelsen är bilden. En befriande bild-konst-kulturteologi*, Stockholm.

Bergmann, S. and Bråkenhielm, C. R. (eds) (1994), *Kontextuell livstolkning. Teologi i ett pluralistiskt Norden*, (Religio 43), Lund.

Bergmann, S. and Bråkenhielm, C. R. (eds) (1998), *Vardagskulturens teologi – i nordisk teologisk tolkning*, Nora.

Bergmann, S. and Eidevall, G. (eds) (1995), *Upptäckter i kontexten. Teologiska föreläsningar till minne av Per Frostin*, (Skrifter från Institutet för kontextuell teologi 3), Lund.

Bernstein, R. J. (1987), *Bortom objektivism och relativism. Vetenskap, hermeneutik och praxis*, Göteborg, (*Beyond Objectivism and Relativism. Science, Hermeneutics and Praxis*, Philadelphia 1983).

Bevans, S. B. (1992), *Models of Contextual Theology*, Maryknoll.

Boff, L. (1993), 'Vad betyder den nya evangeliseringen efter 500 år Latinamerika?', *Svensk Teologisk Kvartalskrift*, vol. 69, 1/1993.

Böhme, G. (1989), *Für eine ökologische Naturästhetik*, Frankfurt am Main.

Böhme, H. (1988), *Natur und Subjekt*, Frankfurt am Main.

Bosch, D. J. (1991), *Transforming Mission. Paradigm Shifts in Theology of Mission*, (American Society of Missiology Series, no. 16), Maryknoll.

Cavalli, A. (1991), 'Soziale Gedächtnisbildung in der Moderne', in Assmann, A. and Harth, D. (eds), *Kultur als Lebenswelt und Monument*, Frankfurt am Main, pp.200-210.

Chomsky, N. (1973), *Aspekte der Syntax-Theorie*, Frankfurt am Main, (*Aspects of the Theory of Syntax*, 1965).

Chung, Hyun Kyung (1992), *Schamanin im Bauch – Christin im Kopf. Frauen Asiens im Aufbruch*, Stuttgart, (*Struggle to be the Sun again. Introducing Asian Women's Theology*, 1990).

Coe, S. (1973), 'In Search of Renewal in Theological Education', *Theological Education*, vol. 9, 4/1973.

Cone, J. (1969), *Black Theology and Black Power*, New York.

Cuomo, C. J. (1998), *Feminism and Ecological Communities. An Ethic of Flourishing*, London and New York.

Curuana, W. (1993), *Aboriginal Art*, London.

Daly, H. E. and Cobb Jr., J. B. (1994), *For the Common Good. Redirecting the Economy toward Community, the Environment, and a Sustainable Future*, 2. enl. ed. Boston.

Daneel, M. L. (1991), 'African Christian Theology and the Challenge of Earthkeeping', *Neue Zeitschrift für Missionswissenschaft*, vol. 47, 2-3/1991, pp.129-142 and pp.225-246.

Duchrow, U. (1993), *Europa i världssystemet 1492-1992. Finns det en väg till rättvisa efter 500 år av plundring, förtryck, penningdyrkan och penningackumulation?* (Skrifter från Institutet för kontextuell teologi 1), Lund, (*Europa im Weltsystem 1492-1992*, 1992).

Duchrow, U. (1994), *Alternativen zur kapitalistischen Weltwirtschaft. Biblische Erinnerung und politische Ansätze zur Überwindung einer lebensbedrohenden Ökonomie*, Gütersloh, (*Alternatives to Global Capitalism*, Utrecht 1995).

Duchrow, U. (1995), 'Kyrkor mellan världsmarknad, världsriken och Guds rike. Biblisk hågkomst och världsekonomiska perspektiv', in Bergmann, S. and Eidevall, G. (eds), pp.20-51.

Duchrow, U. and Gück, M. (1994), *Att hushålla för livets skull. Efter 50 år av dödande fattiggörelse och gränslöst berikande i "Bretton Woods-systemet"*, (Skrifter från Institutet för kontextuell teologi 2), Lund.

Dussel, E. (1993), *Von der Erfindung Amerikas zur Entdeckung des Anderen. Ein Projekt der Transmoderne*, (Theologie Interkulturell 6), Düsseldorf, (*The Invention of the Americas. Eclipse of "the Other" and the Myth of Modernity*, New York 1995).

Ellis, M. H. (1990), *Beyond Innocence and Redemption. Confronting the Holocaust and Israeli Power*, Maryknoll.

Evernden, N. (1987), *Främling i naturen*, (*The Natural Alien*, Toronto 1985).

Foucault, M. (1993), *Diskursens ordning*, Stockholm, (*L'ordre du discours*, Paris 1971).

Frampton, K. (1992), *Modern Architecture. A Critical History*, 3. enl. ed. London 1992.

Frostin, P. (1970), *Politik och hermeneutik. En systematisk studie i Rudolf Bultmanns teologi med särskild hänsyn till hans Luthertolkning*, (Studia Theologica Lundensia 33), Lund.

Frostin, P. (1978), *Materialismus, Ideologie, Religion. Die materialistische Religionskritik bei Karl Marx*, (Studia Theologica Lundensia 37), Lund.

Frostin, P. (1985), 'Kapitalismen kväver kärleken', in Lidman, S., Frostin, P. and Cöster, H. (1985), *Bröd men också rosor*, Stockholm, pp.27-129.

Frostin, P. (1988), *Liberation Theology in Tanzania and South Africa. A First World Interpretation*, (Studia Theologica Lundensia 42), Lund.

Frostin, P. (1992), 'Kristendomens kairos – vågar kyrkorna säga nej till mammon och ja till de fattigas Gud?' in Bergmann, S. (ed) (1992), *De nedtystades Gud. Diakoni för livets skull*, Stockholm, pp.13-53.

Frostin, P. (1994a), *Teologi som befriar. Efterlämnade texter*, (Religio 41), Lund.

Frostin, P. (1994b), *Luther's Two Kingdoms Doctrine. A Critical Study*, (Studia Theologica Lundensia 48), Lund.

Geertz, C. (1973), 'Religion as a Cultural System', in Geertz, C., *The Interpretation of Cultures*, New York, pp.87-125.

Giddens, A. (1992), *The Consequences of Modernity*, 3. ed. Cambridge.

Gregory of Nazianz, 'Oratio 14. De Pauperum Amore', 'Oratio 16' and 'Oratio 18' in *Patrologia ser. graeca*, ed. Migne, vol. 35.

Gustafsson, G. (1995), 'Svenska folket, Estonia och religionen', in Gustafsson, G., *Två undersökningar om Estonia och religionen*, (Religionssociologiska studier 1), Lund, pp.7-46.

Habermas, J. (1988), *Theorie des kommunikativen Handelns. Band 1: Handlungsrationalität und gesellschaftliche Rationalisierung. Band 2: Zur Kritik der funktionalistischen Vernunft*, 4. ed. Frankfurt am Main.

Halbwachs, M. (1985), *Das kollektive Gedächtnis*, Frankfurt am Main.

Hallencreutz, C. F. (1993), *Tredje världens kyrkohistoria. Del I: Från Jesus till det latinamerikanska befrielsekriget*, Uppsala.

Hallman, D. G. (ed) (1994), *Ecotheology. Voices from South and North*, Geneva and New York.

Hofmann, M. (1987), *Bolivien und Nicaragua. Modelle einer Kirche im Aufbruch*, Münster.

Honko, L. (1981), 'Traditionsekologi – en introduktion', in Honko, L. and Löfgren, O. (eds), *Tradition och miljö. Ett kulturekologiskt perspektiv*, Lund.

Hornborg, A. (1992), *Kunskapsfält och forskningsfront i humanekologi*, (unpubl. lecture in Lund 15.10.1992).

Hornborg, A. (1994a), *Ecology As Semiotics. The New Monism and Its Implications for Anthropological Knowledge Construction*, Humanekologiska avdelningen vid Etnologiska institutionen i Lund.

Hornborg, A. (1994b), 'Environmentalism, Ethnicity and Sacred Places. Reflections on Modernity, Discourse and Power', *Canad. Rev. Soc. & Anth.*, vol. 31, 3/1994, pp.245-267.

Hornborg, A. (1998), 'Encompassing Encompassment. Identity, Economy, and Ecology', in Hornborg, A. and Kurkiala, M. (eds), *Voices of the Land. Identity and Ecology in the Margins*, (Lund Studies in Human Ecology 1), Lund, pp.17-33.

Hume, L. (1988), 'Christianity Full Circle. Aboriginal Christianity on Yarrabah Reserve', in Swain, T. and Rose, D. B. (eds), *Aboriginal Australians and Christian Missions. Ethnographic and Historical Studies*, (Australian Association for the Study of Religions 6), South Australia, pp.250-262.

Huppenbauer, M. (1993), 'Philosophical Remarks on the Project of Human Ecology', in Steiner, D. and Nauser, M., pp.99-104.

Irarrázaval, D. (2000), *Inculturation. New Dawn of the Church in Latin America*, Maryknoll.

Irvin, D. T. (1994), 'Contextualization and Catholicity. Looking Anew for the Unity of the Faith', *Studia Theologica*, vol. 48, 2/1994, pp.83-96.

Jeanrond, W. G. (1995), 'Att reflektera över Gud idag', *Svensk Teologisk Kvartalskrift* 4/1995, pp.171-176.

John, O. (1988), 'Die Tradition der Unterdrückten als Leitthema einer theologischen Hermeneutik', *Concilium*, vol. 24, 6/1988, pp.519-526.

John, O. (1991), 'Fortschrittskritik und Erinnerung. Walter Benjamin, ein Zeuge der Gefahr', in Arens, E., John, O. and Rottländer, P., *Erinnerung, Befreiung, Solidarität. Benjamin, Marcuse, Habermas und die politische Theologie*, Düsseldorf, pp.13-80.

Kairos Central America. A Challenge to the Churches of the World, (1988), New York.

1992 *Kairos Declaration of the Peoples' Parliament:* http://www.c3.hu/~bocs/pofp/declarat.htm .

Kairos Europe, European Kairos Document – For a socially just, life-sustaining and democratic Europe, (1998), Heidelberg, (Swedish translation: http://members.tripod.com/~IKT/kairos.html).

Kairos South Africa, (Swedish translation: *Sanningens ögonblick för Sydafrika. Kairosdokumentet: En utmaning för kyrkan – en teologisk kommentar till den politiska krisen i Sydafrika*, (KISA) Uppsala 1986), (*Challenge to the church. A theological comment on the political crisis in South Africa; the Kairos document and commentaries*, Geneva 1985).

Kairos Sverige, (1989), *Missionsorientering*, vol. 143, 2/1989. (English translation: *Kairos Sweden. Invitation to a Swedish Kairos Process*, Lunds stift and Institutet för kontextuell teologi, Lund 1991).

Kairos USA. On The Way: From Kairos to Jubilee, (1994), Kairos USA, Chicago.

Kairos Zimbabwe, (1999), Harare.

Kasper, W. (1985), 'Tradition als theologisches Erkenntnisprinzip', in Löser, K., Lehmann, K. and Lutz-Bachmann, M. (eds), *Dogmengeschichte und katholische Theologie*, Würzburg, pp.376-403.

King, U. (ed) (1995), *Religion and Gender*, Oxford.

Kippenberg, H. G. (1991), *Die vorderasiatischen Erlösungsreligionen in ihrem Zusammenhang mit der antiken Stadtherrschaft. Heidelberger Max-Weber-Vorlesungen 1988*, Frankfurt am Main.

Klappert, B. (1994), *Versöhnung und Befreiung. Versuche, Karl Barth kontextuell zu verstehen*, Neukirchen-Vluyn.

Købke Sutton, G. (1986), 'Noldes nadver. En kunstners beretning', *Louisiana Revy*, vol. 27/2, pp.34-35.

Kristiansen, R. E. and Ruus, O. C. (1996), 'Religion og kontekstualitet', in Kristiansen, R. et al., *Religion i kontekst. Bidrag til en nordnorsk teologi*, (KULTs skriftserie 49), Oslo, pp.5-45.

Kuhn, T. S. (1978), *Die Struktur wissenschaftlicher Revolutionen*, 3. ed. Frankfurt am Main, (*The Structure of Scientific Revolutions*, Chicago 1962).

Kurtén, T. (1987), *Grunder för kontextuell teologi. Ett wittgensteinskt sätt att närma sig teologin i diskussion med Anders Jeffner*, Åbo.

Limouris, G. (ed) (1990), *Justice, Peace and the Integrity of Creation. Insights from Orthodoxy*, Geneva.

Link, C. (1989), 'Die Transparenz der Natur für das Geheimnis der Schöpfung', in Altner, G. (ed), *Ökologische Theologie. Perspektiven zur Orientierung*, Stuttgart, pp.166-195.

Lloyd, J. (1991), *German Expressionism. Primitivism and Modernity*, New Haven and London.

Lohfink, G. (1993), *Wem gilt die Bergpredigt? Zur Glaubwürdigkeit des Christlichen*, Freiburg, Basel and Wien.

Lohfink, N. (1987), *Das Jüdische am Christentum. Die verlorene Dimension*, Freiburg, Basel and Wien.

Maxwell, N. (1992), 'What Kind of Inquiry Can Best Help Us Create a Good World?', *Science, Technology & Human Values*, vol. 17, no. 2, pp.205-227.

McFague, S. (2001), *Life Abundant. Rethinking Theology and Economy for a Planet in Peril*, Minneapolis.

Merchant, C. (1989), *Ecological Revolutions. Nature, Gender and Science in New England*, Chapel Hill and London.

Metz, J. B. (1972), 'Erinnerung des Leidens als Kritik eines teleologisch-technologischen Zukunftsbegriffs', *Evangelische Theologie*, vol. 32, pp.338-352.

Moltmann, J. (1989), *Der Weg Jesu Christi. Christologie in messianischen Dimensionen*, München.

Moltmann-Wendel, E. (1993), 'Rückkehr zur Erde', *Evangelische Theologie*, vol. 53, pp.406-420.

Nolan, A. (1995), 'What Is Contextual Theology? A South African Perspective', in Bergmann and Eidevall (eds), pp.10-19.

Park, C. C. (1994), *Sacred Worlds. An Introduction to Geography and Religion*, London and New York.

Persson, P. E. (1971), *Att tolka Gud idag. Debattlinjer i aktuell teologi*, Lund.

Pétursson, P. (1995), 'Kyrka, folkreligion och nyreligiösitet i postmodern kontext', in Bergmann and Eidevall (eds), pp.73-97.

Picht, G. (1989), *Der Begriff der Natur und seine Geschichte*, Stuttgart.

Primavesi, A. (2000), *Sacred Gaia. Holistic Theology and Earth System Science*, London and New York.

Rappaport, R. A. (1979), *Ecology, Meaning, and Religion*, Berkeley.

Relph, E. (1976), *place and placelessness*, London.

Rorty, R. (1992), *Der Spiegel der Natur. Eine Kritik der Philosophie*, 2. ed. Frankfurt am Main, (*Philosophy and the Mirror of Nature*, Princeton 1980).

Rorty, R. (1993), *Kontingenz, Ironie und Solidarität*, 2. ed. Frankfurt am Main, (*Contingency, Irony, and Solidarity*, Cambridge 1989).

Sandström, S. (1993), 'För fantasin står alla dörrar öppna. Om förnuftets komplementaritet och kreativitet', in Berefelt, G. (ed), *Den barnsliga fantasin*, (Centrum för barnkulturforskning 22), Stockholm, pp.85-119.

Sandström, S. (1995), *Intuition och åskådlighet*, Stockholm.

Scherpe, K. R. (ed) (1988), *Die Unwirklichkeit der Städte. Großstadtdarstellungen zwischen Moderne und Postmoderne*, Hamburg.

Schreiner, L. (1989), 'Kontextuelle Theologie', *Evangelisches Kirchenlexikon Band 2*, Göttingen, pp.1418-1422.

Schreiter, R. J. (1985), *Constructing Local Theologies*, London.

Sennett, R. (1995), *Fleisch und Stein. Der Körper und die Stadt in der westlichen Zivilisation*, Berlin, (*Flesh and Stone*, New York and London 1994).

Sheldrake, P. (2001), *Spaces for the Sacred. Place, Memory and Identity*, London.

Shiva, V. (1991), *Staying Alive. Women, Ecology and Development*, 4. ed. London and New Jersey.

Sjölin, J.-G. (1993), *Att tolka bilder*, Lund.

Sölle, D. (1971), *Politische Theologie. Auseinandersetzung mit Rudolf Bultmann*, Stuttgart.

Sölle, D. (1990), *Gott denken. Einführung in die Theologie*, Stuttgart.

Steiner, D. (1993), 'Human Ecology as Transdisciplinary Science', in Steiner and Nauser (eds), pp.47-76.

Steiner, D. and Nauser, M. (eds) (1993), *Human Ecology. Fragments of anti-fragmentary views of the world*, London and New York.

Stockton, E. (1995), *Aboriginal Spirituality. A Gift to the Nation*, Alexandria, Australia.

Ströter-Bender, J. (1991), *Zeitgenössische Kunst der 'Dritten Welt'*, Köln.

Takenaka, M. (1995), *The Place Where God Dwells. An Introduction to Church Architecture in Asia*, Hongkong.

Tanner, K. (1997), *Theories of Culture. A New Agenda for Theology*, Minneapolis.

Tergel, A. (1991), *Kyrkan och Tredje Världen*, Stockholm.

Tillich, P. (1956), *Systematische Theologie Band I*, 2. ed. Stuttgart.

Tinker, G. E. (1993), *Missionary Conquest. The Gospel and Native American Cultural Genocide*, Minneapolis.

Tracy, D. (1985), 'Theological Method', in Hodgson, P. C. and King, R. (eds), *Christian Theology. An Introduction to Its Traditions and Tasks*, 2. ed. Philadelphia, pp.35-60.

Tracy, D. (1986), 'Abschließende Gedanken zur Konferenz. Einigkeit mitten in Verschiedenheit und Konflikt', in Küng, H. and Tracy, D. (eds), *Das neue Paradigma von Theologie. Strukturen und Dimensionen*, Zürich and Gütersloh, pp.233-242.

Tracy, D. (1994), 'The Return of God in Contemporary Theology', *Concilium* 6/1994, pp.37-46.

von Uexküll, J. and Kriszat, G. (1983), *Streifzüge durch die Umwelten von Tieren und Menschen. Bedeutungslehre*, new ed. Frankfurt am Main (1970).

Ungunmerr-Baumann, M.-R. (1984), *Australian Stations of the Cross*, Melbourne.

Wägner, E. and Tamm, E. (1985), *Fred med jorden*, new ed. Knivsta 1985, (Stockholm 1940).

Warren, K. J. (1993), 'A Feminist Philosophical Perspective on Ecofeminist Spiritualities', in: Adams, C. J. (ed), *Ecofeminism and the Sacred*, New York, pp.119-132.

WCC Canberra 1991, *World Council of Churches Seventh Assembly, Canberra, Australia, 7-20 february 1991*, (Swedish translation in *Kom, Heliga Ande! – Canberra 1991*, (Tro & Tanke, 1991:9), Uppsala, pp.67-110).

Weibel, P. (ed) (1994), *Kontext Kunst*, Köln.

Welsch, W. (1995), *Grenzgänge der Ästhetik*, Leipzig and Stuttgart.

Wiedenhofer, S. (1990), 'Tradition', in *Geschichtliche Grundbegriffe. Historisches Lexikon zur politisch-sozialen Sprache in Deutschland*, Band 6, Stuttgart, pp.607-650.

Index